101 GORGEOUS EARRINGS

Martingale®
& COMPANY

Credits

President & CEO • Tom Wierzbicki

Publisher • Jane Hamada

Editorial Director • Mary V. Green

Managing Editor • Tina Cook

Technical Editor • Dawn Anderson

Copy Editor • Marcy Heffernan

Design Director • Stan Green

Production Manager • Regina Girard

Illustrator • Robin Strobel

Cover & Text Designer • Shelly Garrison

Photographer • Brent Kane

Mission Statement

Dedicated to providing quality products
and service to inspire creativity.

101 Gorgeous Earrings
© 2008 Martingale & Company

Martingale®
& C O M P A N Y

Martingale & Company®
20205 144th Ave. NE
Woodinville, WA 98072-8478 USA
www.martingale-pub.com

Printed in China
13 12 11 10 09   8 7 6 5 4 3 2

**Library of Congress
Cataloging-in-Publication Data
is available upon request.**

ISBN: 978-1-56477-889-5

Scrapbook papers used in book design:

- Adorn It Carolee's Creations: New Year's Collection, Sunshine Party Designs

- Basic Grey: Blush, Charmed BLU 654; Blush, Charmed BLU 654; Lilykate, Rain LIK 555; Mellow, Juicy, MEL 892; Stained Glass/Orange Peel FRU 604; Stella Ruby, Clouds in the Park STE 731; Stella Ruby, London Sunset STE 728; Two Scoops, Blueberry Custard TSC 1049; Two Scoops, Mint Chocolate Chip TSC 1050

- Deja Views: Fresh Print, Blue Raspberry Collage

- EK Success Ltd.: Nostalgiques, Blue plaster RSNAP010

- Fancy Pants Designs, Inc.: Bluebell 837 by Nancie Rowe-Janitz; Sweet Nothings 851 by Nancie Rowe-Janitz

- Flair Designs: Paradise Collection, Tropical Sunset

- K & Company: Classic K McKenna Green Linen Flat Paper 643077 667360; Yellow Texture Flat Paper 643077 645189

- Memory Box, Inc.: Homespun Collection

- My Mind's Eye: Bohemia, Barefoot Birthday, Floral/Turquoise BH1070; Bohemia Bliss, Love of My Life, #BH2050; Bohemia Bungalow, Our Family, Medallion/Light Orange #BH2158; Kaleidoscope, On the Shore, Dots/Mint Paper # KS3071; Magnolia, Starburst Girly Girl, Dots/Light Blue MG1049

- Paper Adventures: Blue Linen Wash by Linda Maron

TABLE OF CONTENTS

INTRODUCTION

Earrings make a great fashion statement and are a perfect way to express your personal style. They are quick to make and require very few tools. With 101 earring projects for inspiration, there's too much temptation to resist. You'll want to make a different pair for every outfit! Make several in an afternoon, and make some extras to give as gifts. Once you get started you won't want to stop!

You'll find the projects and materials lists together for easy reference. The basic techniques, tools, and supplies for making earrings are included in "Earring Basics" on page 56. Most projects require only basic tools, which you'll find listed in "Earring Basics." A few projects, however, require specialty tools or supplies, which are listed at the end of the materials lists for those projects. Detailed project instructions, with illustrations as necessary, are located at the back of the book and will guide you each step of the way.

Get inspired, have fun, and make some great earrings!

THE PROJECTS

PEARL AND CRYSTAL CHANDELIERS
By Paulette Biedenbender

Shimmering pearls and crystals dangling from delicate chandelier earring findings add just the right touch for elegant evening wear.

MATERIALS

Instructions on page 60.

2 silver-finished chandelier earring findings:
Rings and Things

10 Crystal AB2x 4 mm Swarovski crystal bicones

2 Black Diamond AB 4 mm Swarovski crystal bicones

22 Vintage Rose 4 mm Swarovski crystal pearls

18" of sterling silver 24-gauge half-hard wire

8 sterling silver 24-gauge 1½" head pins

2 silver ear wires

CHERRY QUARTZ
AND TURQUOISE DANGLES
By Susan Johnston

A bead cap with six open flower-like petals provides the perfect opportunity for attaching the turquoise dangles.

MATERIALS

Instructions on page 60.

2 cherry quartz 12 x 17 mm faceted oval rounds

2 turquoise 5 mm disc spacers

12 turquoise 4 mm rounds

2 sterling silver 12 mm openwork flower-style bead caps

4 sterling silver 5 mm daisy spacers

28 sterling silver 2 mm rounds

2 sterling silver 20-gauge 2" head pins

12 sterling silver 24-gauge 1½" head pins

2 sterling silver lever-back ear wires

TURQUOISE TRAPEZOIDS
By Susan Johnston

Alternate spacers and rounds to cover the wrapping wire for any similar large, flat bead where the hole runs the width of the bead. If you make the wire-wrapped loop large enough, it can be used to make a matching pendant!

MATERIALS

Instructions on page 60.

2 turquoise 1⅛" long trapezoids

24 sterling silver 2 mm rounds

20 sterling silver 4 mm daisy spacers

10" of non-tarnish silver 24-gauge craft wire, cut in half

2 sterling silver ear wires

SHIMMERS OF TURQUOISE
By Susan Johnston

Stack bead caps in graduated sizes for a true designer look! The largest bead cap has eight open flower-like petals, ideal for attaching dangles.

MATERIALS

Instructions on page 60.

2 turquoise 7 mm rounds

2 turquoise 4 mm rounds

16 turquoise 3 mm rounds

36 sterling silver 2 mm rounds

2 sterling silver 6 mm large-holed bead caps

2 sterling silver 8 mm flat snowflake-style bead caps

2 sterling silver 12 mm flower-style bead caps

2 sterling silver 3 mm daisy spacers

6 sterling silver 4 mm daisy spacers

2 sterling silver 5 mm daisy spacers

16 sterling silver 24-gauge 1½" head pins

2 sterling silver 20-gauge 2" head pins

2 sterling silver lever-back ear wires

RED BEADS AND BALI FINDINGS
By Susan Johnston

Customize these stylish yet simple earrings by changing the bead color to match a specific outfit! Be sure to use a colored bead that is small enough to nestle down into the Bali bead.

MATERIALS

Instructions on page 60.

4 red 4 mm rounds

2 sterling silver 8 mm Bali beads

4 sterling silver 2 mm rounds

2 sterling silver 20-gauge 2" head pins

2 sterling silver ear wires

GOLDEN HESSONITE WITH OVAL LOOP

By Elizabeth Erickson

The oval ring in this design is from a chain. When working with chain, save scraps and odd links to use in other projects. If you use both base-metal and precious-metal chain, keep them separate. It is easy to get them mixed up.

MATERIALS

Instructions on page 61.

6 hessonite 5 x 10 mm faceted nuggets

2 gold-filled 6 x 10 mm oval links from a chain

2 gold vermeil 26-gauge 1½" Bali head pins with granulated ball heads

2 gold vermeil ear wires: Rishashay

ORANGE, OLIVE, AND PINK LAMPWORK

By Elizabeth Erickson

These beautiful lampworked beads call for simple findings. The brushed gold is a good choice if you want a muted look. Try out different findings by holding them up to the finished component before you make your decision. Usually one finding will stand out as the best choice.

MATERIALS

Instructions on page 61.

2 orange, olive, and pink 12 mm lampworked beads: AnneMarie Herrlich (Bobby Bead)

4 brushed gold 4 mm bead caps

2 gold-filled 2.5 – 3 mm rounds

2 gold-filled 24-gauge 1½" head pins

2 gold-filled ear wires

Jeweler's cement (optional)

GOLD FOIL RECTANGLES
By Elizabeth Erickson

These foil beads closely mimic the appearance of fine Italian glass from the island of Murano, but they come from Indonesia and only look expensive.

MATERIALS

Instructions on page 61.

2 gold foil 14 x 16 mm rectangles

2 gold-filled 2.5 mm rounds

2 gold vermeil 3 mm Bali spacers

2 gold-filled 22-gauge 1½" head pins

2 gold vermeil Bali ear wires: Rishashay

BRONZE-COLORED FANCY COINS AND PEARLS
By Elizabeth Erickson

The rich look of the metallic Czech bead calls for gold findings. They are not much more expensive than good sterling findings and greatly add to the overall design.

MATERIALS

Instructions on page 61.

2 bronze 13 mm Czech colored glass coins with a metallic finish

4 bronze 7 mm faceted pearls

2 gold vermeil 3.5 – 4 mm Bali spacers

1¼" or more of gold-filled 2 mm cable chain (allow extra chain to compensate for links lost when making cuts)

4" of gold-filled 24-gauge half-hard wire

2 gold 26-gauge 1½" Bali head pins with granulated ball heads

2 gold vermeil Bali ear wires

FACES OF EASTER ISLAND

By Leslie Pope

The red-and-green tones in the lampworked bead echo the subtle tones found in the face pendant.

MATERIALS

Instructions on page 61.

2 ceramic 1³⁄₈" top-holed face pendants: Twisted Sistah Beads

2 lampworked 10–12 mm glass beads

4 sterling silver 2 mm daisy spacers

2 sterling silver 10 mm jump rings

6" of sterling silver 18-gauge half-hard wire, cut in half

2 sterling silver ear wires

BRASSY AND BOLD

By Paulette Biedenbender

To maintain a unified look, coordinate the three colors of seed beads to the tones found in the raku bead.

MATERIALS

Instructions on page 61.

4 brass affirmation rings (Hope, Love, Believe, and Dream): Vintaj

2 raku beads, 12 x 5 mm coins

Two 4 mm cubes

Two 4 mm cylinders

16 size 8 seed beads; 8 in one color, 4 in a second color, and 4 in a third color

10 brass 21-gauge 4 mm jump rings

12 brass 21-gauge 2" head pins

2 brass ear wires

MOOKITE WITH AFRICAN TRADE BEAD DANGLE

By Elizabeth Erickson

A simple finding can pull together the elements of your earrings. Here, the shape of a crimp bead echoes the pattern of the trade bead.

MATERIALS

Instructions on page 62.

2 mookite 15 mm faceted squares

2 striped 10 mm African trade bead rondelles

2 jade 5 mm rough-cut rondelles

4 sterling silver 7 mm flat discs

2 sterling silver 2 x 3 mm crimp beads

3" of sterling silver 22-gauge half-hard wire, cut in half

2 sterling silver 26-gauge 1½" ball head pins

A few seed beads that will fit inside the trade bead

2 sterling silver Bali ear wires

BLISTER PEARL HOOPS

By Paulette Biedenbender

Satin-like blister pearls, bugle beads, and seed beads are easily strung on beading wire in a delicate roundabout design. The iris finish on the bugle beads is a perfect match for the iridescent pearl.

MATERIALS

Instructions on page 62.

2 copper 12 x 17 mm blister pearls

1 gram metallic gold iris 3 mm bugle beads

2 dark copper size 8 seed beads: Toho (Bobby Bead)

1 gram dark copper size 11 seed beads: Toho (Bobby Bead)

26" of .010, 19-strand flexible beading wire (No substitutions. Earring needs to be extremely flexible.)

2 gold 1 x .050 mm crimp tubes

2 gold ear wires

DARK BLUISH GREEN CRYSACOLA RECTANGLES
By Elizabeth Erickson

Notice the dark areas on the spacers. Silver that is oxidized has a very earthy look and is great for combining with dark, rich-colored stones.

MATERIALS

Instructions on page 62.

2 crysacola (chrysocolla) 15 x 20 mm rectangles

4 sterling silver 2.5 mm rounds

4 sterling silver 4 mm Bali spacers

2 sterling 22-gauge 1½" head pins

2 sterling silver Bali ear wires

CAT'S-EYE STRIPES
By Elizabeth Erickson

When it comes to silver, consider the wide range of options available. The almost cloudy quality of these matte bead caps works well with the sky colors in the lampworked bead. You can create a longer drop by starting the wrap farther from the bead to allow for more wraps.

MATERIALS

Instructions on page 62.

2 blue, green, and black 12 mm lampworked beads

2 matte sterling silver 2.5 mm rounds

4 matte sterling silver 7 mm bead caps

2 sterling silver 22-gauge 1½" ball head pins

2 sterling silver lever-back ear wires

KYANITE RECTANGLE WITH DANGLE

By Elizabeth Erickson

Kyanite is a very beautiful stone. The more you look at it, the more you will love how varied the subtle colors are. The width of the top rectangle bead calls for a wider ear wire, such as these double-spiral ear wires.

MATERIALS

Instructions on page 62.

2 kyanite 13 x 18 mm rectangles

2 kyanite 7 x 13 mm rectangles

3½" of sterling silver 22-gauge half-hard wire, cut in half

2 sterling silver 22-gauge 1½" spiral head pins: Bobby Bead

2 sterling silver Bali ear wires: Bobby Bead

KYANITE AND ICE

By Elizabeth Erickson

The decorated post has a nice oxidized pattern on it that brings out the muddiness of the square kyanite bead. Matte sterling silver rounds were used to bring out the matte detail in the earring post.

MATERIALS

Instructions on page 63.

2 kyanite 14 mm squares

2 kyanite 7 mm rondelles: Scottsdale Bead Supply

4 matte sterling silver 4 mm rounds

2 sterling silver 20-gauge 1½" head pins

2 sterling silver decorated posts: Nina Designs

DREAMSICLE

By Yvonne Irvin

For a creative twist, photo anchors, intended for scrapbooking, were incorporated into this earring design.

MATERIALS

Instructions on page 63.

Two 20 mm posies: My Elements

2 orange 12 mm lampworked discs

4 salmon 6 mm freshwater pearls

2 black-and-white 4 mm Czech rounds

2 white size 11 seed beads

4 salmon small photo anchors

1½" or more of 2 mm flat cable chain, cut in half (allow extra chain to compensate for links lost when making cuts)

10 sterling silver 22-gauge 4 mm jump rings

4 sterling silver 20-gauge 1" head pins

2 sterling silver ear wires

ROSIE

By Yvonne Irvin

The small dangles at the bottom of the earring feature a unified color scheme, but the elements of each vary slightly, adding a touch of playfulness.

MATERIALS

Instructions on page 63.

2 rose-and-black 10 mm lampworked beads

2 rose 13 mm Venetian tabs

6 Light Rose 4 mm Swarovski crystal bicones

8 black onyx 2 mm rounds

4 sterling silver 15 mm curved tubes

2 polished pewter 8 mm spiral tabs

8 sterling silver 4 mm bicones

2 sterling silver 20-gauge 3 mm jump rings

2 sterling silver 20-gauge 4 mm jump rings

8 sterling silver 22-gauge 1" head pins

4 sterling silver 20-gauge 1½" eye pins

2 sterling silver ear wires

BLACK ONYX RECTANGLES
By Elizabeth Erickson

Black onyx is a simple, inexpensive, but elegant-looking stone. Mixed with these geometric shapes, it takes on more of an edgy look.

MATERIALS

Instructions on page 63.

2 black onyx 13 x 18 mm rectangles: The Bead Monkey

2 black onyx 12 x 13 mm V-shaped beads: The Bead Monkey

2 sterling silver 6 x 9 mm Bali diamond-shaped beads: Bobby Bead

3" of sterling silver 20-gauge half-hard wire, cut in half

2 sterling silver 24-gauge 1½" ball head pins

2 sterling silver ear wires: Nina Designs

PINK COIN PEARLS
By Elizabeth Erickson

Coin pearls are available in every color imaginable. This is a versatile size and can be used in earrings, bracelets, and necklaces. The flat spiral design of both the head pin and ear wire help to continue the shape of the coin throughout.

MATERIALS

Instructions on page 63.

2 fuchsia 12–13 mm coin-shaped freshwater pearls

2 sterling silver 2–2.5 mm rounds

2 sterling silver 3 mm spacers

2 sterling silver 22-gauge 1½" spiral head pins: Bobby Bead

2 sterling silver ear wires: Bobby Bead

KIWI JASPER AND BLACK ONYX

By Paulette Biedenbender

Geometric differences create a pleasant flow in either an upside-down or right-side-up fashion statement.

MATERIALS

Instructions on page 63.

4 kiwi jasper 14 x 14 mm puffed squares

8 black onyx 8 mm puffed coins

4 sterling silver 5 mm daisy spacers

8" of sterling silver 22-gauge, half-hard wire, cut in half

2 sterling silver 22-gauge 2" head pins

2 sterling silver ear wires

AMAZONITE RECTANGLES WITH BLACK ONYX DROPS

By Elizabeth Erickson

The amazonite beads with bands of dark brown, black, beige, and aqua are reminiscent of a seascape. The designer imagined sand beaches with wildflowers growing nearby and tried to evoke that image in the design.

MATERIALS

Instructions on page 63.

2 amazonite 14 x 18 mm rectangles

6 black onyx 4 mm faceted rounds

2 sterling silver 9 mm flower-shaped beads

4 sterling silver 2.5 mm rounds

8 sterling silver 4 mm plain spacers

5½" of sterling silver 22-gauge half-hard wire

2 sterling silver 24-gauge 1½" ball head pins

2 sterling silver Bali ear wires

LARGE GREEN TURQUOISE BALLS

By Elizabeth Erickson

These fun earrings have lots of swing. The weight of the bead along with the length of the connector gives this design movement. The grape cluster connector is as wide as the turquoise bead, which helps balance the earring.

MATERIALS

Instructions on page 64.

2 green 15 mm turquoise rounds

2 sterling silver 15 mm Bali grape cluster connectors: Bobby Bead

2 sterling silver 22-gauge 1½" head pins with twisted rope heads: Bobby Bead

2 sterling silver ear wires: Bobby Bead

GREEN RIBBED JADE

By Elizabeth Erickson

The rough-cut fluorite beads with subtle color variations were chosen to complement the matte quality of the translucent carved jade beads. The ribbed wirework design on the ear wire creates an integrated look.

MATERIALS

Instructions on page 64.

2 jade 15 mm "ribbed" diamond-shaped beads: Silk Road Treasures

6 fluorite 4–5 mm rough-cut rondelles

2 sterling silver 4 mm daisy spacers

2 sterling silver 3.5 mm daisy spacers

2 sterling silver 24-gauge 1½" ball head pins

2 sterling silver ear wires: Nina Designs

STERLING NOODLES AND SHIMMERING CRYSTALS

By Paulette Biedenbender

Sterling tubes and crystal bicones create a frame around center crystal drops. The subtle smoky tones in the Black Diamond crystals are similar to the sterling tubes, creating a monochromatic color scheme.

MATERIALS

Instructions on page 64.

2 Black Diamond 6 mm Swarovski crystal bicones

12 Black Diamond 3 mm Swarovski crystal bicones

8 sterling silver 2 x 16 mm curved noodles

8 sterling silver 3 mm daisy spacers

6 sterling silver 4 mm jump rings

2 silver 1 x .050 mm crimp tubes

10" of .010 flexible beading wire, cut in half (no substitute)

2 sterling silver 24-gauge 1½" head pins

2 sterling silver ear wires

FRESHWATER COIN PEARLS AND CRYSTALS

By Paulette Biedenbender

The satiny smoothness of pearl and the dazzle of crystal is all it takes for simply tailored drops.

MATERIALS

Instructions on page 64.

2 white 12 mm coin-shaped freshwater pearls

2 Black Diamond 6 mm Swarovski crystal bicones

2 sterling silver 3 mm daisy spacers

2 sterling silver 24-gauge 2" head pins

2 sterling silver ear wires

HAMMERED SILVER HOOPS
By Clara Walker for Nina Designs

Simple and contemporary, hammered ovals dangle from the center of hammered hoops.

MATERIALS

Instructions on page 64.

2 sterling silver 11.9 x 9.4 x 5.2 mm flat hammered-finish ovals: Nina Designs

2 silver 44.3 x 29.3 x 2.4 mm hammered-finish circles with center cutouts: Nina Designs

2 sterling silver .9 x 5 mm soldered jump rings: Nina Designs

2 sterling silver 36.5 x .5 x .5 mm head pins: Nina Designs

2 sterling silver ear wires: Nina Designs

SATURN MOONS
By Leah Rivers for Nina Designs

Combining the same materials in different shapes adds interest to a design. Here freshwater potato pearls and coin-shaped pearls are paired.

MATERIALS

Instructions on page 64.

2 white 12–12.5 mm coin-shaped freshwater pearls: Nina Designs

2 white 5–5.5 mm freshwater potato pearls: Nina Designs

2 silver 25 mm flat hammered-finish circle links with holes on opposite sides: Nina Designs

4 sterling silver 36 x .5 x .5 mm ball head pins: Nina Designs

2 sterling silver ear wires: Nina Designs

RED LEATHER
By Elizabeth Erickson

The square decoration on the ear wire repeats the straight lines of the leather bead, and the earring works equally well without the connector. The leather bead makes these earrings extremely lightweight.

MATERIALS

Instructions on page 64.

2 red 10 x 20 mm leather rectangles: The Bead Monkey

2 sterling silver 20 mm coiled connectors with open loops

2 sterling silver 26-gauge 2" head pins

2 sterling silver ear wires: Nina Designs

Jeweler's cement (optional)

BROWN CARVED JASPER LANTERNS
By Elizabeth Erickson

Jasper is easier to carve than most stones. As a result, it comes in many wonderful shapes and sizes and is still quite reasonably priced.

MATERIALS

Instructions on page 64.

2 jasper 15 mm carved barrels: Scottsdale Bead Supply

2 jade 2–3 mm rough-cut rondelles

2 sterling silver 4 mm twisted wire spacers

2 sterling silver 24-gauge 1½" head pins with twisted wire heads

2 sterling silver ear wires

Jeweler's cement (optional)

SQUARES AND SILVER
By Elizabeth Erickson

Look beyond the color of the bead when choosing findings. Here, the texture around the edge of the bead is repeated in the spacer and ribbed melon bead. Hold up different earring components to the bead before making a final selection.

MATERIALS

Instructions on page 65.

2 Czech 15 mm squares

2 stone chips

2 sterling silver 5 x 9 mm melons

2 sterling silver 4 mm Bali spacers

2 sterling silver 24-gauge 2" ball head pins

2 sterling silver ear wires

CARNELIAN CARVED OVALS
By Elizabeth Erickson

Have fun combining different geometric shapes. Here the triangle gives a tapered end to the elongated circle. The interesting shapes on the triangle bead are echoed in the decorated head pins.

MATERIALS

Instructions on page 65.

2 carnelian 20–25 mm oval-shaped rings

2 peridot 3–4 mm faceted rondelles

2 sterling silver 9 mm Bali triangles

4 sterling silver 3–4 mm Bali daisy spacers

2½" of sterling silver 22-gauge half-hard wire, cut in half

4 sterling silver 24-gauge 1½" Bali 4-dot head pins

2 sterling silver lever-back ear wires

IRIDESCENT SHELL DOUGHNUT WITH PEARL DANGLE
By Elizabeth Erickson

These are fun and very light earrings. The possible combinations of beads, connectors, and pearls are endless.

MATERIALS

Instructions on page 65.

2 shell 20 mm round doughnuts

6 chartreuse 5 mm pearls

2 sterling silver decorative links: Bobby Bead

4 sterling silver 3.5–4 mm Bali daisy spacers

2 sterling silver 24-gauge 1½" head pins (for top)

4 sterling silver 24-gauge 1½" ball head pins (for bottom)

2 sterling silver ear wires: Bobby Bead

YELLOW AND BLUE TURQUOISE
By Elizabeth Erickson

Because these earrings combine several different geometric shapes, silver findings with granulated dots were used to create a cohesive design.

MATERIALS

Instructions on page 65.

2 yellow turquoise 14 mm coins

2 turquoise 5 x 7 mm barrels

4 sterling silver 4 mm Bali spacers: Bobby Bead

2 sterling silver 22-gauge 2" Bali head pins with 6 mm pyramid heads: Bobby Bead

2 sterling silver ear wires: Bobby Bead

PAUA OVALS
By Elizabeth Erickson

The paua shell has a wide range of colors. Look for a Swarovski crystal that picks up one of the colors in the shell.

MATERIALS

Instructions on page 65.

2 paua shell 14 x 18 mm flat ovals

4 Pacific Opal 4 mm Swarovski crystal bicones

2 sterling silver 26-gauge 2" Bali granulated teardrop head pins: Rishashay

2 sterling silver ear wires

TWO RINGS WITH DANGLE
By Elizabeth Erickson

The texture of the hammered ring mimics the faceting of the rondelles, while the round shape of the rings is repeated in the balls on the ear wire and head pin. The repetition of elements creates a unified design.

MATERIALS

Instructions on page 65.

4 apatite 4–5 mm faceted rondelles

2 peridot 3 mm rondelles

4 labradorite 3 x 4 mm brick-shaped beads with an AB finish

2 sterling silver 14–18 mm soldered rings

2 sterling silver 16-gauge 6–8 mm jump rings

2 sterling silver 24-gauge 1½" ball head pins

2 sterling silver ear wires

CONTEMPO CHARM
By Yvonne Irvin

To maintain balance in this multicolored earring, place the bead colors evenly throughout.

MATERIALS

Instructions on page 65.

2 anodized aluminum 10 mm barrels
2 green 10 mm angel wings
2 black 8 mm saucers
2 black 4 mm saucers
2 charteuse 8 mm faceted, rough-cut rounds
2 purple-lined 5 mm rounds
4 pink 3 mm rounds
2 charteuse 3 mm faceted rounds
2 orange 7 mm faceted doughnuts
2 striped (E) seed beads
8 size 11 seed beads
2 Blue Zircon 5 mm Swarovski crystal bicones
6 Sapphire 4 mm Swarovski crystal bicones
Two 4 mm Swarovski cubes
2 pewter 8 mm swirl beads
2 sterling silver 3 mm rounds
4 sterling silver 2 mm rounds
4 sterling silver 3 mm spacers
1½" or more of silver 4 mm flat cable chain, cut in half (allow extra chain to compensate for links lost when making cuts)
2" of silver 2 mm flat cable chain, cut in half (allow extra chain to compensate for links lost when making cuts)
16 sterling silver 20-gauge 1½" head pins
4½" of sterling silver 20-gauge half-hard wire, cut in half
2 sterling silver ear wires

ON A ROLL
By Yvonne Irvin

Create a whimsical pair of earrings by turning dice into beads. Use an adjustable power drill and a ¹⁄₁₆" drill bit to create the holes.

MATERIALS

Instructions on page 66.

1 pair black standard-sized dice (drilled through center)
Two lampworked 8 x 12 mm Czech beehives
Two 4 mm Swarovski bicones
1 orange 4 mm Czech round
1 chartreuse 4 mm Czech round
2 sterling silver 3 mm disks
2 sterling silver 2 mm rounds
2 sterling silver 20-gauge 1½" head pins
2 sterling silver 20-gauge 1½" eye pins
2 sterling silver ear wires

CONICAL SWIRL

By Yvonne Irvin

Start with a wire coil to make this dynamic cone shape. Experiment with different colors of craft wire.

MATERIALS

Instructions on page 66.

24" of yellow 18-gauge wire, cut in half: Artistic Wire

2 decorated, clear 8 mm rounds

2 black 4 mm rounds

2 sterling silver 20-gauge 1½" head pins

2 sterling ear wires

DANCING DISC

By Yvonne Irvin

The zigzag beads that dangle from the discs give visual movement to the earrings. Changing the placement of the bicone colors on each earring adds a bit of whimsy.

MATERIALS

Instructions on page 66.

2 lampworked 20 mm discs

2 pewter 5 x 12 mm zigzag beads

Four 4 mm Swarovski crystal bicones (2 each of 2 different colors)

2 sterling silver 3 mm rounds

2 pewter 4 mm spacers

2 sterling silver 20-gauge 1½" head pins

2 sterling silver 20-gauge 1½" eye pins

2 sterling silver ear wires

LOTUS BLOSSOMS

By Jess Italia-Lincoln

Look to nature for inspiration in your designs. An intricately detailed filigree envelopes genuine jadeite and is combined with blue fluorite to resemble the budding lotus blossoms of water gardens.

MATERIALS

Instructions on page 66.

2 green 10 mm jadeite rounds

2 blue 6 mm fluorite rounds

2 natural brass 12 mm filigree bead caps: Vintaj

2 natural brass 6 mm daisy bead caps: Vintaj

6 natural brass 7.25 mm jump rings: Vintaj

2 natural brass 21-gauge 2" head pins: Vintaj

2 natural brass 15 x 20 mm round loop ear wires: Vintaj

ETERNITY BUTTERFLY GARDENS

By Jess Italia-Lincoln

Etched Vintaj eternity garden rings are adorned by fancy filigree butterflies, brilliant Swarovski crystals, and handmade Unicorne glass, which dance freely and capture light.

MATERIALS

Instructions on page 66.

2 Light Goldenrod 4 x 8 mm borosilicate glass doughnuts: Unicorne Beads

2 Lime 4 mm Swarovski crystal bicones

2 Pacific Opal AB 2 x 4 mm Swarovski crystal bicones

4 Satin Smoked Topaz 4 mm Swarovski crystal bicones

4 Smoked Topaz 3 mm Swarovski crystal bicones

2 natural brass 25 mm eternity garden rings: Vintaj

2 natural brass 13 x 14 mm filigree butterfly charms: Vintaj

4 natural brass 19-gauge 4.75 mm jump rings: Vintaj

4 natural brass 18-gauge 5.25 mm jump rings: Vintaj

8 natural brass 24-gauge 1½" pearl head pins: Vintaj

2 natural brass 21-gauge 1" eye pins: Vintaj

2 natural brass 10 x 20 mm ear wires: Vintaj

RING AROUND THE PERFECT PEARL

By Wendy Mullane

Pretty pearls are tucked gently into ornate Vintaj bead caps and adorned by hammered and etched brass rings—a fun and playful design you can create in many colors!

MATERIALS FOR EARRINGS

Instructions on page 67.

2 aqua 7 mm freshwater pearls

2 natural brass 22 mm hammered rings: Vintaj

2 natural brass 7.5 mm filigree bead caps: Vintaj

4 natural brass 19-gauge 4.75 mm jump rings: Vintaj

2 natural brass 15-gauge 9.5 mm etched jump rings: Vintaj

2 natural brass 24-gauge 1½" head pins: Vintaj

2 natural brass 15 x 20 mm round loop ear wires: Vintaj

FIRE AND ICE

By Mackenzie Mullane

Within the shadows of this delicate crest filigree are reflections of cool crystal, hot orange, and bright blue. These stunning earrings are sure to turns heads!

MATERIALS FOR EARRINGS

Instructions on page 67.

2 Crystal 9 x 18 mm Swarovski crystal faceted drops

2 Turquoise AB 2 x 6 mm Swarovski crystal bicones

4 Fire Opal 4 mm Swarovski crystal bicones

2 natural brass 28 x 33 mm crest filigree: Vintaj

6 natural brass 19-gauge 4.75 mm jump rings: Vintaj

6 natural brass 21-gauge 1" head pins: Vintaj

2 natural brass 21-gauge 1½" eye pins: Vintaj

2 natural brass 15 x 20 mm round loop ear wires: Vintaj

STONES AND DIAMONDS
By Leslie Pope

Match the stone chips to the colors found in the ceramic pendant to create color balance in your design. For a more rustic take on these earrings, use copper wire and copper ear wires instead of silver.

MATERIALS

Instructions on page 67.

2 ceramic ¾" top-holed diamond pendants: Marsha Neal Studio

4 stone chips

2 size 11 seed beads

8" of sterling silver 20-gauge half-hard wire, cut in half

2 sterling silver ear wires

GOLDEN PEARLS AND CLAY
By Leslie Pope

Pearls come in a variety of colors. Choose a color that picks up hues from the pendant.

MATERIALS

Instructions on page 67.

2 ceramic 8 x 20 mm top-holed rectangular pendants: Marsha Neal Studio

Two 5 mm freshwater pearls

4 size 11 seed beads

8" of sterling silver 20-gauge half-hard wire, cut in half

2 sterling silver ear wires

CORAL SPIRAL CHANDELIERS
By Rita Briant

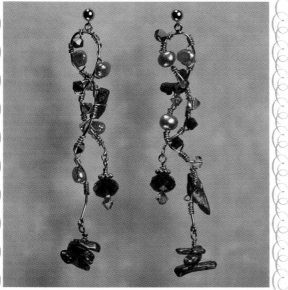

Coral chips and soft orange freshwater pearls along with a sprinkling of crystals enhance these gold spiral earring findings. Make the earrings alike or slightly different as shown. You may want to line your beads up ahead of time to make a pleasing color arrangement.

MATERIALS

Instructions on page 67.

1 set 14kt gold-filled double-spiral chandelier earring components with loops: Turtle Island Beads

8 – 12 red 10 – 12 mm coral chips

6 – 10 light orange 4.5 – 5 mm freshwater pearls

7 – 12 Dark Red Coral 4.5 mm Swarovski crystal bicones

8 – 12 Crystal Brandy 4.5 mm Swarovski crystal bicones

2 Siam 8 mm Swarovski crystal domed spacers

2 gold 5 mm daisy spacers

40" of 14kt gold-filled 24-gauge dead-soft wire

4 gold-filled 1½" x .021" head pins

Two 14kt gold-filled earring posts

GOLDEN AUTUMN
By Rita Briant

An antique gold-plated pewter leaf charm is the base for an array of fall-colored crystals with a cluster drop. This pattern allows for random selection and placement of the 3 mm Swarovski crystal bicones. The leaf drop is also available in antique silver-plated pewter.

MATERIALS

Instructions on page 68.

2 antique gold-plated pewter 20 x 25 mm filigree leaf drops: Turtle Island Beads

44 to 48 of fall color mix* 3 mm Swarovski crystal bicones

6" of 14kt gold-filled 24-gauge dead-soft wire, cut in half

50" of 14kt gold-filled 28-gauge dead-soft wire, cut in half

7 links of 14kt gold-filled rolo chain

Ten 14kt gold-filled 1½" x .021 head pins

Two 14kt gold-filled ear wires

If a fall color mix is not available, choose from the following Swarovski crystal colors: Siam, Olivine, Smoked Topaz, Indian Red, Crystal Copper, Crystal Golden Shadow, Light Topaz, Crystal Chili Pepper.

AMBER, JET, AND CORAL DROPS
By Elizabeth Erickson

When making the wire triangle to hold the teardrop dangle, strive to create the shape of a garment hanger.

MATERIALS

Instructions on page 68.

2 coral 22 mm teardrops

4 jet or black glass 7–8 mm rondelles

2 amber 7–9 mm rough-cut flat squares

5" of sterling silver 24-gauge half-hard wire, cut in half

3" of sterling silver 22-gauge half-hard wire, cut in half

2 sterling silver lever-back ear wires

BIRDS WITH GARNET
By Elizabeth Erickson

The garnet beads beautifully capture the colors found in the ceramic coin. The round shape of the stone set into the ear wires is repeated in the dangle for balance. When you find beads you love, buy them, even if you don't have a clear idea of how you can use them. The garnet beads shown on these two pages came from the same strand of beads, purchased long ago.

MATERIALS

Instructions on page 68.

2 ceramic 15 mm decorative coins

2 garnet 6 x 8 mm flat diamonds

2 garnet 4 mm rounds

2 matte sterling silver 2.5 mm rounds

2 sterling silver 7 mm Bali Saturn-shaped spacers

2 sterling silver 4.5 mm Bali spacers

3" of sterling silver 22-gauge half-hard wire, cut in half

2 sterling silver 22-gauge 1½" head pins

2 sterling silver ear wires with garnet settings: Bobby Bead

LABRADORITE DOUGHNUTS WITH GARNET CLUSTER

By Elizabeth Erickson

The garnet cluster was a great find. You can substitute any other unique bead. To keep the design unified, match the color of the 4 mm round used in the center of the doughnut to the color of the bead used for the dangle.

MATERIALS

Instructions on page 68.

2 labradorite 25 mm doughnuts

2 garnet 10–12 mm clusters or other uniquely shaped bead

2 garnet 4 mm rounds

2 sterling silver 4 mm Bali decorative spacers

5½" of sterling silver 22-gauge half-hard wire, cut in half

2 sterling silver 24-gauge 1½" ball head pins

2 sterling silver 24-gauge plain 1½" head pins

2 sterling silver ear wires

SILVER COINS WITH BRONZE PEARLS AND GARNET DROPS

By Elizabeth Erickson

Making a wire loop just the right size takes practice. On dangle earrings in particular, you want the loop to be big enough for the earring components to swing freely but not so big as to compromise the strength of the loop. These loops are about 3.5 mm in diameter.

MATERIALS

Instructions on page 69.

2 sterling silver 13 mm coins

2 bronze 7 mm faceted pearls

4 sterling silver 4–5 mm Bali spacers

4 garnet 4 mm rounds

3" of sterling silver 22-gauge half-hard wire, cut in half

2 sterling silver 24-gauge 1½" ball head pins

2 sterling silver ear wires with garnet settings: Bobby Bead

CHAIN MAIL
By Melissa Rediger

The graduated silver jump rings, along with the iridescent bead, give these earrings a contemporary feel. Carefully open the jump rings to maintain their shape.

MATERIALS

Instructions on page 69.

2 bluish green 5 x 13 mm lampworked beads

2 silver 18-gauge 10 mm jump rings

4 silver 18-gauge 7 mm jump rings

4 silver 18-gauge 5 mm jump rings

2 silver 18-gauge 3.5 mm jump rings

2 sterling silver ear wires

GREEN TOURMALINE FRINGE
By Nina Cooper for Nina Designs

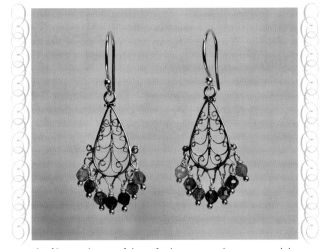

The filigree design of these findings gives them a very delicate feel. Use beads in a single color family for a monochromatic look or mix colors as desired.

MATERIALS

Instructions on page 69.

14 green 3 mm tourmaline faceted rounds: Nina Designs

2 sterling silver 14 x 23 mm filigree teardrop earring findings with ruffled lower edge: Nina Designs

14 sterling silver 36 x .5 x .5 mm 1" ball head pins: Nina Designs

2 sterling silver ear wires: Nina Designs

PINK TOURMALINE FRINGE
By Nina Cooper for Nina Designs

The tiny dot design in the filigree finding is repeated in the ear wires and head pins for a unified look. These earrings would look great with pearl dangles as well.

MATERIALS

Instructions on page 69.

24 pink 3 mm tourmaline faceted rounds: Nina Designs

2 sterling silver 23 x 27 mm round filigree earring findings with ruffled lower edge: Nina Designs

24 sterling silver 36 x .5 x .5 mm ball head pins: Nina Designs

2 sterling silver ear wires: Nina Designs

PURPLE LAMPWORKED BEADS
By Melissa Rediger

The subtle variations in the tourmaline dangles echo the colors in the lampworked bead. The dangles add nice movement to the earring.

MATERIALS

Instructions on page 69.

2 purple 9 x 15 x 15 mm lampworked beads

16 tourmaline 3–3.5 mm faceted rondelles

4 sterling silver 2.5 mm spacers

½" or more of sterling silver 2 mm round link chain cut in half (allow extra chain to compensate for links lost when making cuts)

14 sterling silver 26-gauge 1½" eye pins

2 sterling silver 24-gauge 1½" eye pins

2 sterling silver ear wires

BASKETWEAVE
By Janice Berkebile

To create the antique finish shown here, use liver of sulfur on the silver, following the manufacturer's instructions.

MATERIALS

Instructions on page 69.

Allow extra wire for making flush cuts on wire ends.

2 olive 8 mm faceted freshwater pearls

1 taupe 8 mm freshwater pearl

1 brown 8 mm freshwater pearl

1 dark brown 6 mm freshwater pearl

1 shell 6 mm freshwater pearl

10 sterling silver 18-gauge 4 mm jump rings

12¼" of sterling silver 18-gauge dead-soft wire

12" of sterling silver 24-gauge dead-soft wire

6 sterling silver 24-gauge 1½" ball head pins

2 sterling silver ear wires

SPECIALTY TOOLS AND SUPPLIES

Chasing hammer

Liver of sulfur

Polishing cloth

Steel bench block and pounding pad

Steel wool (0000)

SPIRALS
By Janice Berkebile

The hammered finish on these simple spirals adds interest and texture. Using ear wires with ball ends adds one more element to the design.

MATERIALS

Instructions on page 70.

Allow extra wire for making flush cuts on wire ends.

5" of sterling silver 18-gauge dead-soft wire, cut in half

6" of sterling silver 24-gauge dead-soft wire

2 sterling silver ear wires

SPECIALTY TOOLS AND SUPPLIES

Chasing hammer

Liver of sulfur

Polishing cloth

Steel bench block and pounding pad

Steel wool (0000)

LOOP DE LOOP VINES
By Janice Berkebile

LOOP DE LOOP SUNRAYS
By Janice Berkebile

The loops are made in varying places on the round-nose pliers, which accounts for the differences in size.

MATERIALS

Instructions on page 70.

Allow extra wire for making flush cuts on wire ends.

2 olive 8 mm faceted freshwater pearls

2 shell 6 mm freshwater pearls

2 Colorado Topaz AB2x 3 mm Swarovski crystal bicones

2 sterling silver decorative bead caps that fit over the 8 mm pearls

6" of sterling silver 18-gauge dead-soft wire, cut in half

6 sterling silver 24-gauge 1½" ball head pins

2 sterling silver ear wires

SPECIALTY TOOLS AND SUPPLIES

Chasing hammer

Liver of sulfur

Long round-nose pliers

Polishing cloth

Steel bench block and pounding pad

Steel wool (0000)

The form for this ornate earring starts out as a horizontal line of loops, which is shaped into a circle, making this project much easier than it appears.

MATERIALS

Instructions on page 71.

Allow extra wire for making flush cuts on wire ends.

2 lime 10 mm freshwater pearls

4 dark brown 4 mm freshwater pearls

4 Colorado Topaz AB2x 6 mm Swarovski crystal bicones

2 sterling silver decorative caps that fit the 10 mm pearls

4 sterling silver 18-gauge 4 mm jump rings

14¼" of sterling silver 18-gauge dead-soft wire

10 sterling silver 24-gauge 1½" ball head pins

2 sterling silver ear wires

SPECIALTY TOOLS AND SUPPLIES

Chasing hammer

Liver of sulfur

Long round-nose pliers

Polishing cloth

Steel bench block and pounding pad

Steel wool (0000)

SILVER DOTS
By Elizabeth Erickson

The small silver bead carries the silver dot theme throughout the earring.

MATERIALS

Instructions on page 71.

2 metallic 12 mm coins

2 sterling silver 3 mm Bali daisy spacers

2 sterling silver 2–2.5 mm rounds

2 sterling silver 22-gauge 1½" head pins

2 sterling silver lever-back ear wires

PURPLE AND SAGE RECTANGLES WITH SPIRAL FINDINGS
By Elizabeth Erickson

The spiral shape is carried throughout the earring and helps create an integrated look. It takes a while to build up a variety of good-quality findings. They add so much to your designs. A great-looking finding can make an inexpensive bead look extraordinary.

MATERIALS

Instructions on page 72.

2 stone 15 x 20 mm flat rectangles

2 jade 3–4 mm rough-cut rondelles

2 sterling silver 3.5–4 mm Bali spacers

2 matte sterling silver 2.5 mm rounds

2 sterling silver 22-gauge 2" head pins with spiral heads

2 sterling silver spiral ear wires

BUTTERFLIES

By Trish Kirkham

The Golden Shadow crystals have a slight gold cast to them, making them a wonderful complement to the gold tones used elsewhere in this earring.

MATERIALS

Instructions on page 72.

2 butterfly beads

4 black 6 mm faceted rounds

4 Golden Shadow 6 mm Swarovski crystal bicones

4 Maroon 6 mm Swarovski crystal pearls

2 gold-filled 2 mm rounds

2.5" or more of gold-filled 2.7 mm diamond-cut curb chain (14 links total; allow extra chain to compensate for links lost when making cuts)

14 gold-filled 24-gauge 2" head pins

2 gold-filled ear wires

CHAROITE NUGGETS

By Elizabeth Erickson

Stone nuggets sandwiched between ornate Bali spacers are suspended from silver chains. Using chain with links of different shapes and sizes enhances this interesting design.

MATERIALS

Instructions on page 72.

2 charoite 18 mm rough-cut nuggets

4 sterling silver 7 mm Bali spacers

4 matte sterling silver 2.5 mm rounds

6" or more of sterling silver 2 mm chain, cut into four equal pieces (allow extra chain to compensate for links lost when making cuts)

2 sterling silver 18-gauge jump rings

3" of sterling silver 24-gauge half-hard wire, cut in half

2 sterling silver ear wires

BLUEBIRDS
By Jean Yates

Wire more of the beads for each earring onto the front of each chain for a fuller look, but keep the beads low, leaving around ¾" of chain on each earring exposed, thereby adding to the fluffy look around each bird.

MATERIALS

Instructions on page 72.

2 ceramic Sea Bird Terra Trinkets: Earthenwood Studio

14 light sapphire 4 x 6 mm fire-polished Picasso rondelles: Fusion Beads

2" or more of sterling silver 3.2 mm dangle chain, cut in half (allow extra chain to compensate for links lost when making cuts): Fusion Beads

2 sterling silver 6 mm Snapeez jump rings: Via Murano

14 sterling silver 24-gauge 1½" head pins: Fusion Beads

2 sterling silver lever-back ear wires: Fusion Beads

ENAMEL CONES
By Paulette Biedenbender

Chains enhanced with crystals and cubes easily sway from enamel cones. The crystal bicones add a touch of sparkle.

MATERIALS

Instructions on page 72.

2 enamel 7 x 21 mm cones: C-Koop Beads available from Bead Needs

16 matte raku blue-and-teal 4 mm cubes: Toho (Bobby Bead)

24 White Opal AB 4 mm Swarovski crystal bicones

8 Crystal AB 4 mm Swarovski crystal bicones

2 sterling silver 4 mm rounds

2 sterling silver 2 mm rounds

12" or more of silver 1.5 x 2 mm oval-link chain (allow extra chain to compensate for links lost when making cuts)

24" of sterling silver 24-gauge half-hard wire

8 sterling silver 24-gauge 1½" head pins

2 sterling silver ear wires

FULL MOON THROUGH BRANCHES
By Jean Yates

The hammered ear wires replicate the faceting of the crystal chatons. Both are great light reflectors, making these earrings sparkle!

MATERIALS

Instructions on page 73.

2 white 12–13 mm coin pearls: Fusion Beads

8 crystal 6 mm chatons (rhodium-plated chain links): Fusion Beads (cut the links connecting them but keep the two loops, one on each end)

8 white 3 mm Swarovski crystal pearls: Fusion Beads

2 sterling silver twig links: Fusion Beads

20 sterling silver 2 mm seamless rounds: Fusion Beads

8 sterling silver 4 mm jump rings: Via Murano

10 sterling silver 26-gauge 1½" head pins

2 sterling silver 21 x 4.4 x .9 mm shiny hammered-finish ear wires: Nina Designs

VICTORIANA
By Jean Yates

The ornate patterns on the silver findings tie them together. The crystals add a pale touch of color, but keep the earrings neutral for versatility.

MATERIALS

Instructions on page 73.

2 sterling silver 14 x 14 x 6 mm Thai cast beads with marcasite: Nina Designs

2 sterling silver 12.2 x 12.2 x 2 mm twisted links: Nina Designs

4 Silk 6 mm Swarovski crystal rounds

2 sterling silver 6 mm Snapeez jump rings: Via Murano

2 sterling silver 72.3 x 9.8 x 2.8 mm decorative head pins: Nina Designs

2 sterling silver and marcasite 18.5 x 18.5 x 4.7 mm hoops: Nina Designs

SLANTED DOORS
By Leah Rivers for Nina Designs

Hammered silver ear wires are the perfect complement to the hammered square links in this contemporary design. Carnelian stones add a punch of color.

MATERIALS

Instructions on page 73.

4 carnelian 4–6 mm faceted rondelles: Nina Designs

2 silver 20 mm flat hammered square links: Nina Designs

2 silver 16 mm flat hammered square links: Nina Designs

2 silver 12 x 13 x 5 mm patterned squares with diagonal holes: Nina Designs

2½" or more of sterling silver 1.5 x 1.5 mm chain with round, smooth links (allow extra chain to compensate for links lost when making cuts): Nina Designs

6" of sterling silver 24-gauge dead-soft wire: Nina Designs

2 sterling silver 26-gauge 1" ball head pins: Nina Designs

2 sterling silver 21 x 4.4 x .9 mm shiny hammered-finish ear wires: Nina Designs

HORSESHOE NAIL DANGLES
By Cristi Johnson

Not just for horses—make these earrings from horseshoe nails for your favorite horse rider.

MATERIALS

Instructions on page 73.

4 SB5-1.95" horseshoe nails (purchased at farm supply store)

4 RN4.5-1.76" horseshoe nails

4 nickel-plated 20-gauge 4 x 6 mm oval jump rings

10 nickel-plated 20-gauge 3 x 4 mm oval jump rings

8' of colored 24-gauge craft wire, cut in half

2 sterling silver ear wires

glue (quick drying to hold nails together for wrapping)

ORANGE BALL AND CRYSTALS
By Melissa Rediger

The yellow and orange tones in the crystal bicones pick up the colors in the round orange bead, making them perfect coordinates.

MATERIALS

Instructions on page 74.

2 orange 10 mm etched rounds

6 Fire Opal AB 4 mm Swarovski crystal bicones

2 brushed sterling silver 23 mm rings

4 sterling silver 3 mm spacers

8 sterling silver 24-gauge 1½" head pins

2 sterling silver ear wires

GREEN NUGGETS
By Melissa Rediger

The brushed silver rings make a lovely frame for the smooth green focal stones.

MATERIALS

Instructions on page 74.

When making your bead selection, be sure that the nugget and two rondelles will fit in a straight line through the center of the silver ring, allowing just enough space for the wraps on the wrapped loops.

2 chrysoprase 12 mm nuggets

4 citrine 3.5 mm faceted rondelles

2 brushed sterling silver 23 mm rings

3" of sterling silver 24-gauge dead-soft wire, cut in half

2 sterling silver ear wires

CHAIN AND BEADS
By Tracy Stanley

Pearls, crystals, glass, or stone beads work well together in these colorful dangles.

MATERIALS

Instructions on page 74.

Two 6–8 mm beads

26 total assorted 4–5 mm beads (2 matching groups of 13 beads each)

6 links of sterling silver 1.7 mm bar-and-link chain (links are about 12 mm long)

6" of sterling silver 24-gauge dead-soft wire, cut in half

26 sterling silver 1½" x .022" ball head pins

2 sterling silver ear wires

SPECIALTY TOOLS AND SUPPLIES

Liver of sulfur

Polishing cloth

Steel wool (0000)

BEAD WITH CLUSTER ON TOP
By Tracy Stanley

The beaded cluster at the top of this earring looks great when it protrudes slightly over the edges of the bead below, resembling an oversized bow on top of a package.

MATERIALS

Instructions on page 74.

2 sterling silver 10 mm patterned squares

24 total assorted 3–5 mm beads (2 matching groups of 12 beads each)

2 sterling silver 18-gauge 2½" ball head pins

24 sterling silver 1½" x .022" ball head pins

2 sterling silver ear wires

SPECIALTY TOOLS AND SUPPLIES

Liver of sulfur

Polishing cloth

Steel wool (0000)

WIRE FRAME WITH A SPIRAL
By Tracy Stanley

The rice-shaped freshwater pearls are the perfect shape to dangle inside this wire frame. The color of the pearls closely matches the wire, creating a neutral earring that can be worn with any outfit!

MATERIALS

Instructions on page 74.

Allow extra wire for making flush cuts on wire ends.

2 silver 10–12 mm rice-shaped freshwater pearls

2 Bali silver 4 mm daisy spacers

2 sterling silver 7 mm jump rings

16" of sterling silver 16-gauge dead-soft wire, cut in half

2 sterling silver 18-gauge 1½" ball head pins

2 sterling silver lever-back ear wires

SPECIALTY TOOLS AND SUPPLIES

Chasing hammer

Liver of sulfur

Polishing cloth

Steel bench block and pounding pad

Steel wool (0000)

PEARL CUPS
By Tracy Stanley

The cups for these earrings were formed with silver discs using a dapping block and punch. Bead caps are a great substitute if you choose not to make the cups yourself.

MATERIALS

Instructions on page 75.

2 white 8 mm pearls

8 white 4 mm potato-shaped freshwater pearls (holes drilled through the narrowest width)

8 sterling silver 24-gauge ½" discs: Rio Grande

2" or more of sterling silver 3 x 4 mm oval-link chain, cut in half (allow extra chain to compensate for links lost when making cuts)

6" of sterling silver 24-gauge dead-soft wire, cut in half

8 sterling silver 24-gauge 1½" ball head pins

2 sterling silver lever-back ear wires with open rings

SPECIALTY TOOLS AND SUPPLIES

Dapping block and punches

Liver of sulfur

Polishing cloth

Screw down metal hole punch: Beaducation

Steel wool (0000)

SILVER, AQUA, AND LAVENDER LEAF
By Cassie Barden

To add more motion to the earrings, keep the wire around the leaf bead slightly loose.

MATERIALS

Instructions on page 75.

2 aqua 6 mm translucent faceted beads

2 lavender 8 x 13 mm glass leaf beads

4 sterling silver 4 mm daisy spacers

4 sterling silver 24-gauge 2" eye pins

2 sterling silver ear wires

CHAROITE AND TURQUOISE
By Elizabeth Erickson

These earrings are elegant in their simplicity. The deep, almost muddy eggplant purple of Russian charoite makes the bright turquoise bead pop. Two plain discs are used to create a little more space between the large and small beads. Experiment during assembly to see if additional spacers enhance the overall design.

MATERIALS

Instructions on page 76.

2 charoite 10 x 12 mm barrels

2 turquoise 6 mm barrels

4 sterling silver 7 mm plain discs: Nina Designs

2 sterling silver 24-gauge 1½" head pins

2 sterling silver ear wires

SIGNS OF SPRING
By Jean Yates

The ceramic components add a unique touch to these earrings. The soft colors complement one another and contribute to a soothing design.

MATERIALS

Instructions on page 76.

2 seafoam "Blossom" message sticks: Earthenwood Studio

2 slate Pixie Beads: Earthenwood Studio

10 apatite chips: Fusion Beads

4 dichroic 6–7 mm rondelles: Artbeads

8" of sterling silver 22-gauge dead-soft wire, cut in half

6 sterling silver 24-gauge 3" head pins

2 sterling silver 3-holed ear wires: Nina Designs

WATCH PART DANGLES
By Jill MacKay

Make time stand still when repurposing watch parts, which are available in stamping stores, craft stores, and online.

MATERIALS

Instructions on page 76.

4 Erinite SBL 3 mm Swarovski crystal bicones

6 Pacific Opal AB2x 4 mm Swarovski crystal bicones

6 Pacific Opal 4 mm Swarovski crystal rounds

2 Tanzanite AB 4 mm Swarovski crystal bicones

2 Smoked Topaz CAL 4 mm crystal spacers

4 Indicolite AB2x 6 mm Swarovski crystal bicones

2 Indicolite 6 mm Swarovski crystal bicones

2 Indicolite 4 mm Swarovski crystal bicones

6 violet 5 x 12 mm 4 petal center hole glass floral beads

1 gram of transparent topaz rainbow size 11 seed beads

2 gold MacKay Collection #JMC0308G bead frames

Watch parts:
- 2 gold wheel bridge sections
- 2 gold 6–8 mm crown wheels
- 2 gold 6–8mm Fourth wheels

12 gold 1.3 mm crimp tubes

2 gold 2.5 mm jump rings

2 gold 4 mm jump rings

15" of .024, 49-strand flexible gold beading wire: Beadalon

2 gold 22-gauge 2" head pins

2 gold tone ear wires

SPECIALTY TOOLS

Crimping pliers

SEDONA SUNSET

By Rita Briant

Twenty-two individual peyote-stitched tubular beads encircle the earring hoops, invoking memories of Southwestern sunsets. Metallic coiled-wire spacers separate the colorful beads. The beads are small and easy to make.

MATERIALS

Instructions on page 77.

4 grams each of size 11 Delicas: #1283 matte transparent caribbean teal, #204 antique beige ceylon, #734 opaque chocolate, #1014 metallic thistle gold iris

12" of sterling silver 24-gauge dead-soft wire

12" of gun metal 24-gauge craft wire

12" of copper 24-gauge craft wire

Fireline beading thread, size D/6 lb.

Size 12 long beading needle

2 sterling silver 2 x 40 mm tube earring hoops: Turtle Island Beads

CRAZY LONG

By Trish Kirkham

Choose a metal that complements the tones found in the beads. Here copper makes a good choice because it repeats the rusty tones found in the agate.

MATERIALS

Instructions on page 77.

2 crazy agate 16 mm coins

2 fancy copper 10 x 14 mm ovals

6 copper 2 mm rounds

2 copper 24-gauge 2" head pins

2 copper 22-gauge 2" eye pins

2 copper ear wires

SUNBURST

By Trish Kirkham

Consider using jewelry findings in nontraditional ways. For these earrings, the loop part of a toggle clasp became the dangle. The beaded detail on the inner edge of the dangle is picked up again in the ball detail of the ear wire.

MATERIALS

Instructions on page 77.

2 loop parts of copper Sunburst toggle clasps

2 copper ear wires

ARTISAN

By Trish Kirkham

The components and assembly of this earring mimic those used for "Red and Mustard Yellow with Black Dots" on page 48. See how different the finished appearance of the earrings is simply because of the beads and findings that were chosen. Follow this same formula to create an infinite number of simple but unique earrings.

MATERIALS

Instructions on page 77.

2 artisan lampworked beads

4 copper 4 mm bead caps

4 copper 2 mm rounds

2 copper 24-gauge 2" head pins

2 copper ear wires

NUTCRACKER
By Elizabeth Erickson

RED AND MUSTARD YELLOW WITH BLACK DOTS
By Elizabeth Erickson

What makes this simple design interesting is the gold X on the bead and the detail in the fleur-de-lis shape in the lever-back ear wire. A decorated ear wire can add interest to simple designs.

MATERIALS

Instructions on page 77.

2 red, gold, and blue 9 mm cubes

2 black onyx 4 mm faceted rounds

2 gold vermeil 3.5–4 mm Bali spacers

2 gold-filled 22-gauge 1½" head pins

2 gold-filled ear wires: Rio Grande

Notice the diamond-shaped design in the bead. Let the overall shape of the bead, as well as the patterns found within the bead, help determine the choice of accessories. If the focus of the earring is a beautiful bead rich with color and texture, consider keeping the findings simple.

MATERIALS

Instructions on page 77.

2 red, gold, and black 10 mm lampworked beads: Anne Marie Herrlich (Bobby Bead)

Four 4 mm Swarovski crystal bicones

4 gold vermeil 4 mm Bali spacers

2 gold-filled 22-gauge 1½" head pins

2 gold-filled lever-back ear wires

Jeweler's cement (optional)

RED BONE TEARDROPS
By Elizabeth Erickson

Keeping elements of a design similar helps tie the components together visually. Here the spiral design on the cones is continued on the ear wires.

MATERIALS

Instructions on page 78.

2 red bone or wood 22–24 mm teardrops

4 turquoise or gaspeite (gasperite) 6 mm rondelles

2 sterling silver 9 x 15 mm Bali cones: Bobby Bead

10" of sterling silver 22-gauge half-hard wire

2 sterling silver ear wires: Bobby Bead

AGATE PICTURE FRAMES
By Elizabeth Erickson

Try to find chain that complements the "picture-frame" focal bead. This large bead and its industrial shape call for a heavier chain. Using ear wires with some width helps to balance the width of the picture-frame beads as well.

MATERIALS

Instructions on page 78.

2 agate 18–20 mm picture frame squares

2 jade 6–8 mm rondelles

1½"–2" or more of sterling silver chunky chain, cut in half (allow extra chain to compensate for links lost when making cuts)

2 sterling silver 18-gauge 7 mm jump rings

2 sterling silver 24-gauge 1½" head pins with rope-and-dot heads

4 sterling silver 24-gauge 1½" head pins

2 sterling silver ear wires

COPPER SWIRLS

By Trish Kirkham

Pairing copper findings with copper beads helps to achieve a unified look.

MATERIALS

Instructions on page 78.

4 Gold 5 mm Swarovski crystal pearls

4 serpentine 4 x 6 mm rondelles

2 copper 8 mm coins with swirl designs

2 copper 22-gauge 2" head pins

2 copper ear wires

LAMPWORK WITH PEARLS

By Trish Kirkham

Using two slightly different yet similar lampworked beads adds interest to this pair of earrings. The pearls nicely repeat the gold dots around the lampworked beads.

MATERIALS

Instructions on page 78.

2 fancy lampworked beads

2 Gold 5 mm Swarovski crystal pearls

4 copper 4 mm flat rope-edge spacers

2 copper 22-gauge 2" head pins

2 copper ear wires

MOTTLED COINS
By Trish Kirkham

Textural spacers add interesting contrast when combined with smooth beads.

MATERIALS

Instructions on page 78.

2 green and brown 10 mm mottled coins

2 Bronze 5 mm Swarovski crystal pearls

4 copper 4 mm flat rope-edge spacers

2 copper 22-gauge 2" head pins

2 copper ear wires

CELTIC
By Trish Kirkham

The diamond shape of the bicone beads is roughly repeated in the Celtic link, creating a harmonious design.

MATERIALS

Instructions on page 78.

2 Jonquil 6 mm Swarovski crystal bicones

2 Olivine 6 mm Swarovski crystal bicones

2 copper 10 mm Celtic links

2 copper 22-gauge 2" head pins

2 copper ear wires

MARTINI AND OLIVE ART BEADS
By Paulette Biedenbender

A little whimsy never hurt anyone, and whimsical is exactly what these earrings are. Great for a party night!

MATERIALS

Instructions on page 78.

1 olive art bead: Jangles

1 martini glass art bead: Jangles

5 Tourmaline 6 mm Swarovski crystal rounds

2 red 4 mm Czech faceted rounds

7" of sterling silver 24-gauge, half-hard wire

3 sterling silver 24-gauge 2" head pins

2 sterling silver ear wires

FANCY BLACK AND RED
By Trish Kirkham

Repeating the black and gold colors from the square beads in the remaining earring components ties the elements together. The crystal bicones add contrast.

MATERIALS

Instructions on page 79.

2 red, gold, and black 16 mm squares

4 black onyx 6 mm rounds

4 Crystal Golden Shadow 6 mm Swarovski crystal bicones

6 gold-filled 2 mm rounds

2" or more of gold-filled 2.7 mm diamond-cut curb chain (12 links total; allow extra chain to compensate for links lost when making cuts)

10 gold-filled 24-gauge 2" head pins

2 gold-filled ear wires

DRAGONS

By Trish Kirkham

The round gold shape is repeated in the pearls, the gold beads, and in the ear wires for a cohesive design.

MATERIALS

Instructions on page 79.

2 black 15 mm square wooden dragon beads with diagonal holes

8 Bronze 4 mm Swarovski crystal pearls

2 gold-filled 2 mm rounds

2" or more of gold-filled 2.7 mm diamond-cut curb chain (12 links total; allow extra chain to compensate for links lost when making cuts)

10 gold-filled 24-gauge 2" head pins

2 gold-filled ear wires

MASKS

By Trish Kirkham

The face bead is the focal point in this earring. To keep the design simple, the round gold bead is repeated on the ear wire.

MATERIALS

Instructions on page 79.

2 black-and-gold 20 x 25 mm triangular face beads

2 gold-filled 3 mm rounds

2 gold-filled 24-gauge 2" head pins

2 gold-filled ear wires

BLUE DOTTED LAMPWORK
By Elizabeth Erickson

The shape of the spacers allows them to stand a bit away from the lampworked bead, letting more of it be exposed. Include some matte sterling beads in your collection. Sometimes that slightly frosted look is just the little detail that can make your earring look unique.

MATERIALS

Instructions on page 79.

2 blue-and-lavender 12 mm lampworked beads: AnnMarie Herrlich (Bobby Bead)

4 sterling silver Saturn-shaped Bali spacers

4 matte sterling silver 2.5–3 mm rounds

2 sterling silver 22-gauge 1½" head pins

2 sterling lever-back ear wires

SHOO CHO JADE WITH DIAMOND CAPS AND LAPIS
By Elizabeth Erickson

The pyramid-shaped head pin was chosen to complement the diamond shapes found on the jade bead.

MATERIALS

Instructions on page 79.

2 shoo cho jade 10 x 20 mm rectangle cubed lantern beads with metal caps

2 rough-cut lapis 4 mm rondelles

2 sterling silver 3.5–4 mm Bali daisy spacers

2 sterling silver 22-gauge 2" Bali dotted pyramid head pins: Bobby Bead

2 sterling silver ear wires

STERLING SILVER AND POLKA-DOT BEADS
By Paulette Biedenbender

With a simple twist of the wrist, square wire acquires a diamond-like cut and becomes a fancy frame for bold polka-dot beads.

MATERIALS

Instructions on page 79.

2 royal polka-dot 12–14 mm disc-shaped beads

2 royal polka-dot 10–12 mm rounds

20" of sterling silver 22-gauge, square, half-hard wire, cut in half

2 sterling silver ear wires

SPECIALTY TOOLS

Pin vise (to hold wire for twisting)

JADE FLOWERS AND LAPIS
By Elizabeth Erickson

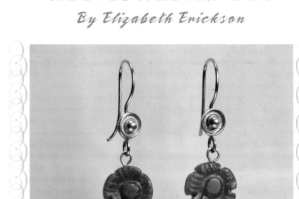

Round shapes are repeated throughout this design, giving diverse elements a coordinated feel. The flower beads add a playful touch, and using faceted rounds, rather than smooth rounds, adds one more element of interest.

MATERIALS

Instructions on page 80.

2 green jade 12 mm flowers

2 lapis 8 mm faceted rounds

2 green jade 5–6 mm rondelles

4 sterling silver 7 mm flat discs

4 sterling silver 2 mm rounds

3¼" of sterling silver 22-gauge half-hard wire, cut in half

2 sterling silver 24-gauge 1½" head pins

2 sterling silver ear wires

EARRING BASICS

TOOLS AND SUPPLIES

The most basic supplies are listed below. A few projects require specialty tools. If a project requires specialty tools, they are listed at the end of the materials list for that project. For instance, crimping pliers are only needed for the "Watch Parts Dangles" on page 45. Flat-nose pliers are not necessary; however, you will need two pairs of pliers to open and close jump rings, so having both chain-nose pliers and flat-nose pliers provides you with pliers for different purposes that can also be used together.

Measuring tape or ruler: You'll need a guide for measuring wire lengths.

Scissors: Use utility scissors, rather than your good scissors, to cut bead-stringing material.

Wire cutters: Used for cutting wire lengths and to trim wire flush with the surface of the project. They can also cut thicker beading wire. Flush-cut cutters leave a smooth edge on the wire.

Chain-nose pliers: Smooth-jawed pliers that taper to a point, used to open and close jump rings, wire loops, and chain without scratching the wire. Because they taper to a point, they work well in small areas.

CAUTION: Use protective eyewear when cutting and working with wire. It is also a good idea to hold the wire on each side of the cutters to prevent loose ends from flying about. When making flush cuts at the end of a piece of wire, cup your hand over the cutter to catch the cut end.

Flat-nose pliers: Smooth-jawed pliers that are squared off at the tips, used for making precise bends in wire. They are also used to open and close jump rings and wire loops.

Round-nose pliers: Pliers with round tapered jaws for creating well-formed loops.

Crimping pliers: Specialized pliers for flattening and securing crimp beads on wire. Chain nose pliers can be substituted but don't create as smooth a crimp.

wire cutters

chain-nose pliers

flat-nose pliers

round-nose pliers

crimping pliers

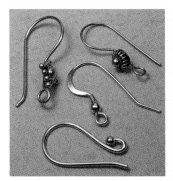

French ear wires

lever-back ear wires

posts

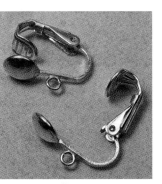

clip-ons

BASIC MATERIALS

Some of the basic materials and findings are covered below.

Earring Findings

Earring findings, available in a variety of metals, are used to attach beaded dangles to the ear. Ear wires are frequently used throughout this book, but posts, hoops, and clip-on findings are also options. Many findings have small loops at the bottom for attaching a dangle. A few styles of findings are shown above but look through the projects in this book for more ideas.

To attach dangles to earring findings, gently open the loop on the earring finding in the same manner as for a jump ring, attach the dangle, and close to secure.

French ear wires: These are hook-shaped wires for pierced ears that can be plain or decorated. Often they have a loop at the bottom for attaching the dangle. Some have a small outward curve at the end that sometimes has a ball end. For this style, string the dangle onto the hook portion and slide it down to the base of the curve. Press the short end of the ear wire against the hook portion to secure the dangle.

Lever-back ear wires: These findings for pierced ears open in the back. Put the front portion of the finding through the ear and secure by pushing the back portion up to meet the front. They can be plain or decorated on the front and have a loop at the bottom for attaching a dangle.

Posts: For pierced ears, these findings have a straight metal pin that is inserted into the ear. The front can have a decorative piece of metal or can be as simple as a ball. The finding is secured on the back of the ear with an ear nut. Posts have a loop for attaching the dangle.

Clip-ons: For non-pierced ears, these findings clip to the ear lobe. Look for clip-on findings with a loop to attach the dangle to. All of the earrings in this book are shown with findings for pierced ears. Clip-on findings can be substituted for posts or ear wires if desired.

Hoops: A variety of hoop styles exist from simple wire to larger-diameter tubing. The tube-style hoops shown on page 46 are for pierced ears, although similar non-pierced styles are available with spring-lever closures. String beads onto the hoop portion of the finding.

Beading Wire

Flexible, nylon-coated beading wires are available in a variety of weights, diameters, materials, and colors. Beading wires often contain 7, 19, 21, or 49 strands of very fine wire; the number of strands affects both the strength and the flexibility of the wire. Match the weight of your beads to the strength of the beading wire and the diameter of the wire to the size of the holes in your beads. Appropriate wire sizes are listed in the materials lists where applicable.

Other Wire

Wire is available in a variety of metals, shapes, and sizes (gauge).

The projects in this book use round wire, unless otherwise specified in the project materials list. The descriptors "half-hard" and "dead-soft" refer to how malleable the wire is at the time of purchase. Half-hard wire is a bit stiffer and can't be reworked very much; dead-soft wire is softer and can take a bit more bending before it becomes brittle and breaks. A smaller gauge has a larger diameter.

Connectors

Jump rings are measured in millimeters and come in different gauges (thickness of the wire). They can be open or soldered shut. Available in a wide range of metals, the jump ring can be selected to match the clasp or other metal materials in the project.

Snapeez rings are open jump rings that close securely with a snap. Available from Via Murano in a variety of materials and sizes, they are more secure than open jump rings.

Crimp Beads or Tube-Shaped Crimp Beads

These hollow beads are tightened on wire to secure clasps and connectors. They are available in a variety of materials, such as gold-filled, sterling silver, and plated base metal. Crimps come in different sizes to accommodate the different sizes of beading wire. The wire you select will determine the size of crimp you will need; this information is often printed on the package. Most crimps used in this book can be flattened with chain-nose pliers, with the exception of the crimps used in "Watch Parts Dangles" on page 45. If you choose to make that project, you'll want to make folded crimps using crimping pliers.

Head Pins (A) and Eye Pins (B)

Available in a variety of metals and sizes, these pins are measured in inches. Eye pins have a plain loop already in place at one end. Head pins can have different designs at the end; plain, flat, round ball, or decorative shapes are available. Match the wire thickness and length with the beads you will be using.

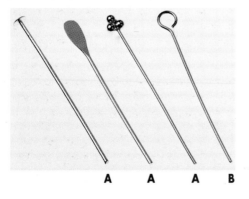

A   **A**   **A**   **B**

How to Turn a Plain Loop

1. Bend the wire at a 90° angle.

2. Using round-nose pliers, grasp the very end of the wire at the point on the tapered jaws that matches the size of loop you wish to create. Rotate the pliers to bend the wire around the lower jaw.

3. Continue bending the wire until the loop is formed.

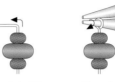

Bend wire 90°.   Wrap wire around the bottom jaw to form a circle.   Form loop on the other end in the opposite direction.

How to Begin and Complete a Wrapped Loop

1. Using round-nose pliers, grasp the head pin or wire approximately ⅛" above the last bead and bend the wire over at a 90° angle.

2. Grasp the wire at the point on the pliers' tapered jaws that matches the size of loop you wish to create. Wrap the end of the wire up and over the top jaw of the pliers.

3. Remove the upper jaw from the loop and reposition the pliers to place the bottom jaw through the loop. Rotate the jaws to bring the wire end all the way around so that it crosses the wire above the beads.

4. Attach the open loop at this time as directed for the individual project. Complete the wrapped loop by winding the wire two to four times around the ⅛" of exposed wire above the beads. Hold the loop with chain-nose pliers and use another pair of pliers to turn the wraps if needed. Keep the wraps close together; if they are a little askew, gently squeeze the wraps together using the tips of the pliers. Trim any excess wire and press the cut end close to the main wire with the pliers.

Bend wire 90°.   Wrap wire over the top of the jaws.   Move to bottom jaw. Wrap wire around to form a circle.   Attach as directed. Wind wire tightly between loop and top bead. Trim.

How to Make a Wire-Wrapped Bail

1. Cut a length of wire as indicated in the project instructions. Center the bead on the wire and bend the wire as indicated in the project instructions. The wires should cross at the top of the bead creating an "X".

2. Using chain-nose pliers, bend one of the wires straight up (vertically) over the center top of the bead and bend the other wire horizontally so it is perpendicular to the first wire.

3. Wrap the horizontal wire a couple of times around the vertical wire and trim the excess.

4. Make a wrapped loop in the vertical wire (see page 58), wrapping the wire down to meet the previous wraps. Or, trim the vertical wire about ½" from the top of the coils and turn a plain loop (see page 58).

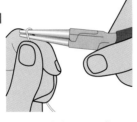

Wrapped loop   Plain loop

How to Make a Tight Wire Coil

1. Begin with a piece of wire with a flush-cut end. Hold the wire vertically in front of you. Grasp the end of the wire in the jaws of your round-nose pliers and rotate your wrist forward to create a loop.

2. Reposition the sire and pliers so the wire extends horizontally in front of you. Continue to coil the wire around the loop until you are about halfway around. Remove the round-nose pliers.

3. Hold the started coil in the jaws of your chain-nose pliers and gently push the wire with your thumb so it follows the curve of the loop. Reposition the pliers and repeat with small movements until the coil reaches the desired size. Always push on the extended wire near the coil. Pushing on the wire further out will result in a sharp bend, rather than a gradual curve.

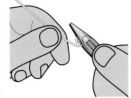

How to Make a Loose Wire Coil

Follow the instructions for "How to Make a Tight Wire Coil" at left, but in steps 2 and 3 maintain more space between the rows of the coil.

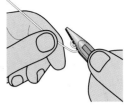

How to Open and Close Jump Rings and Plain Loops

1. Hold the jump ring or plain loop with two pairs of pliers, positioning the gap in the wire between the pliers.

2. Rotate one wrist forward to move the wire away from your body as you rotate the other wrist back toward your body to further open the gap in the wire. Do not pull the wire ends apart from left to right, as this will distort and weaken the ring or loop.

Rotate to open.   Rotate back to close.

How to Harden or Temper Wire

Wire used in jewelry making is usually tempered dead-soft or half-hard so that it can be easily formed into decorative shapes by hand or with hand tools such as pliers. For the wire to permanently retain a certain shape, it needs to be hard tempered. Placing the wire on a hard surface and striking it with a hammer causes the metal molecules to realign, thus hardening the wire. Smooth anvils and striking blocks are used with nylon-faced hammers or rawhide mallets to avoid marring the metal surface.

How to Flatten and Add Texture to Wire

Wire can be flattened and given texture to change the appearance. Place the wire on a steel bench block, cushioned with a pounding pad or old towel, and strike the wire with the broad, nearly flat side of a chasing hammer. A chasing hammer will produce a smooth surface without marking the wire. To add texture to the wire, use the ball peen side of the chasing hammer to strike the wire.

How to Create a Patina Finish on Silver

Liver of sulfur can be used to create a darkened finish on silver wire or jewelry components. Follow the manufacturer's directions to give the finished project or components a patina finish. Then, rub the wire or components with fine steel wool (0000), followed by a polishing cloth. Wire-wrapped pieces will retain a blackened finish in the cracks and crevices, if the antiquing is done after the project is completed.

PROJECT INSTRUCTIONS

Refer to "Earring Basics" on page 56–59 when completing the project instrucions on the following pages.

PEARL AND CRYSTAL CHANDELIERS

Page 5   Length: 2½"

Instructions

1. String onto a head pin: 1 crystal pearl. Turn a plain loop on top. Repeat 2 more times.

2. String onto a head pin: 1 crystal pearl, 1 Black Diamond bicone. Turn a plain loop on top.

3. Cut six 1½" lengths of wire. Turn a plain loop at one end of each length of wire.

4. String onto five of the 1½" wire lengths: 1 crystal pearl, 1 Crystal 2x AB crystal bicone. Turn a plain loop on top of each unit.

5. String onto the remaining 1½" wire length: 2 crystal pearls. Turn a plain loop on top.

6. Gently open the loop on the pearl-and-Black-Diamond unit. Attach the unit to the center of the chandelier earring finding, and close the loop to secure.

7. Open the loop at the pearl end of a pearl-and-crystal unit, attach to the crystal end of a second pearl-and-crystal unit, and close the loop. Open the pearl end of this two-unit piece, attach to the loop on a single pearl, and close the loop.

8. Open the loop at the top of the three-unit piece, attach to a lower-outer loop on the chandelier earring finding, and close the loop.

9. Repeat steps 7 and 8 to add a three-unit piece to the opposite side of the chandelier earring finding.

10. Open the loop at the pearl end of a pearl-and-crystal unit, attach to a loop on the double-pearl unit and close the loop. Open the remaining loop on the double-pearl unit, attach to the loop on a single pearl, and close the loop.

11. Open the loop at the top of the three-unit piece, attach to the lower-center loop on the chandelier earring finding, and close the loop.

12. Attach the dangle to the ear wire.

13. Repeat steps 1–12 to complete the second earring.

CHERRY QUARTZ AND TURQUOISE DANGLES

Page 6   Length: 1¾"

Instructions

1. String onto a 1½" head pin: 1 silver round, 1 turquoise round, and 1 silver round. Begin a wrapped loop on top.

2. String the end of the head pin through an outer hole in a bead cap, and complete the wraps. Add 5 more dangles to the bead cap.

3. String onto a 2" head pin: 1 silver round, 1 daisy spacer, 1 bead cap with dangles, 1 cherry quartz round, 1 daisy spacer, 1 turquoise spacer, and 1 silver round.

4. Make a wrapped loop on top, and then attach the dangle to the ear wire.

5. Repeat steps 1–4 to complete the second earring.

TURQUOISE TRAPEZOIDS

Page 6   Length: 1⅞"

Instructions

1. String 1 turquoise trapezoid onto a piece of wire.

2. String alternately onto each side of the turquoise trapezoid: 6 silver rounds and 5 daisy spacers, starting with a silver round.

3. Cross the wire ends to make an X and complete a wire-wrapped bail with a wrapped loop on top. Attach the dangle to the ear wire.

4. Repeat steps 1–3 to complete the second earring.

SHIMMERS OF TURQUOISE

Page 7   Length: 1⅜"

Instructions

1. String onto a 1½" head pin: one silver round, one 3 mm turquoise round, and one silver round. Begin a wrapped loop on top.

2. String the loop through a hole in a 12 mm bead cap, and complete the wraps.

3. Repeat steps 1 and 2 to add 7 more dangles to the bead cap.

4. String onto a 2" head pin: one silver round, one 3 mm daisy spacer, one 4 mm daisy spacer, one 5 mm daisy spacer, one 7 mm turquoise round, two 4 mm daisy spacers, one bead cap with dangles, one snowflake-style bead cap, one large-holed bead cap, one 4 mm turquoise round, one silver round.

5. Make a wrapped loop on top, and then attach the dangle to the ear wire.

6. Repeat steps 1–5 to complete the second earring.

RED BEADS AND BALI FINDINGS

Page 7   Length: 1¼"

Instructions

String onto a head pin: 1 silver round, 1 red round, 1 Bali bead, 1 red round, 1 silver round. Make a wrapped loop on top, and then attach the dangle to the ear wire. Repeat to complete the second earring.

GOLDEN HESSONITE WITH OVAL LOOP

Page 8   Length: 1⅜"

Instructions

1. String 3 nuggets of varying shades onto a head pin. Begin a wrapped loop.

2. String the loop through an oval chain link and complete the wrap. Attach the dangle to the ear wire.

3. Repeat steps 1 and 2 to complete the second earring.

ORANGE, OLIVE, AND PINK LAMPWORK

Page 8   Length: 1"

Instructions

1. String onto a head pin: 1 bead cap, 1 lampworked bead, 1 bead cap, one gold round. If the bead caps slide around too much, use a dot of jeweler's cement to hold the caps in place.

2. Make a wrapped loop on top, and then attach the dangle to the ear wire.

3. Repeat steps 1 and 2 to complete the second earring.

GOLD FOIL RECTANGLES

Page 9   Length: 1⅛"

Instructions

String onto a head pin: 1 foil rectangle, 1 gold spacer, 1 gold round. Turn a plain loop, and then attach the dangle to the ear wire. Repeat to complete the second earring.

BRONZE-COLORED FANCY COINS AND PEARLS

Page 9   Length: 2⅝"

Instructions

1. Cut the gold-filled chain into 4 equal parts, measuring about 5/16" each. Cut the wire into the following lengths:
   - 2 lengths, each ¾"
   - 2 lengths, each 1¼"

2. String 1 pearl onto a head pin and begin a wrapped loop.

3. String the loop through the last link of a piece of chain and complete the wrap.

4. String a pearl onto a ¾" length of wire and begin a wrapped loop on each end. String one loop through the end link of the chain on the pearl dangle and complete the wrap.

5. String the other loop through the end link of another piece of chain and complete the wrap.

6. Begin a wrapped loop on one end of a 1¼" piece of wire, string the loop through the end link of the chain dangle, and complete the wrap.

7. String 1 Czech bead and 1 spacer onto the wire and make a wrapped loop. Attach the dangle to the ear wire.

8. Repeat steps 2–7 to complete the second earring.

FACES OF EASTER ISLAND

Page 10   Length: 2¼"

Instructions

1. Turn a plain loop at one end of a length of wire. String onto the wire: 1 spacer, 1 glass bead, 1 spacer. Turn a plain loop on top.

2. Gently open a jump ring. String the face pendant and bead unit onto the jump ring and close to secure.

3. Attach the dangle to the ear wire.

4. Repeat steps 1–3 to complete the second earring.

BRASSY AND BOLD

Page 10   Length: 3¼"

Component Construction

1. Trim the head off of two head pins and make a wrapped loop on one end of each.

2. String a raku bead on each trimmed head pin and make a wrapped loop on top. Set aside.

3. Trim the head off of 6 head pins and make a jump ring from each as follows: wrap the head pin around the largest portion of the round nose pliers' jaw, a little more than one complete wrap. Cut one end where the ends overlap with a flush cut. Then cut the other end with a flush cut, so the ends meet.

4. On two head pins string: 1 seed bead, 1 cube, 1 seed bead. Make a wrapped loop on top.

5. On two head pins string: 1 seed bead, 1 cylinder bead, 1 seed bead. Make a wrapped loop on top.

6. Gently open eight 4 mm jump rings. String a seed bead on each and close to secure.

Connecting the Components

1. Gently open a large jump ring and string on a raku bead and an affirmation ring. Close the jump ring. Repeat to connect the opposite side of the raku bead to a second affirmation ring, but before closing the jump ring, string on the bead unit with the cube bead. Close the jump ring.

2. Open a large jump ring. String onto the jump ring: 4 of the 4 mm jump rings with beads, 1 bead unit with a cylinder bead. Do not close the jump ring yet.

3. Attach the large jump ring to the top affirmation ring. Close the jump ring.

4. Open a 4 mm jump ring. String the jump ring through the large jump ring on the top affirmation ring and through the loop of an ear wire. Close to secure.

5. Repeat steps 1–4 to complete the second earring, but attach the cube bead to the top affirmation ring and the cylinder bead and 4 mm jump rings with beads to the bottom affirmation ring.

MOOKITE WITH AFRICAN TRADE BEAD DANGLE

Page 11   Length: 1⅞"

Instructions

1. String onto a head pin: 1 silver disc, 1 trade bead, enough seed beads to fit inside the trade bead (to prevent it from sliding around), 1 silver disc, 1 jade rondelle. Make a wrapped loop on top.

2. Turn a plain loop at the end of one piece of wire. Gently open the plain loop, string on the trade bead dangle, and close the loop to secure.

3. String onto the wire 1 mookite square, 1 crimp bead, but don't crimp! Make a wrapped loop on top, and then attach the dangle to the ear wire.

4. Repeat steps 1–3 to complete the second earring.

BLISTER PEARL HOOPS

Page 11   Length: 2⅛"

Instructions

Refer to the illustration below for steps 2–7.

1. Cut a 13" length of flexible beading wire. Tape the left end of the wire to a work surface (you will work from left to right).

2. String onto the wire: 3 size 11 seed beads.

3. String onto the wire: 1 bugle, 1 size 11 seed bead; repeat 4 more times.

4. String onto the wire: 2 size 11 seed beads, 1 blister pearl, 2 size 11 seed beads.

5. String onto the wire: a total of 5 bugle beads and 4 size 11 seed beads, alternating the beads and starting with a bugle bead.

6. String onto the wire: 3 size 11 seed beads, 1 size 8 seed bead, 3 size 11 seed beads.

7. String onto the wire: a total of 7 bugle beads and 6 size 11 seed beads, alternating the beads and starting with a bugle bead.

8. String onto the wire: 3 size 11 seed beads. Position the portion of the strand on the right side of the pearl, above the pearl as shown.

9. Wrap the right strand (which is now positioned on the left), around to make a small circle and insert the end into the size 8 seed bead and the size 11 seed bead directly to the left of it (right to left direction). See illustration below.

10. Insert the strand on the left into the size 8 seed bead and the size 11 seed bead directly to the right of the size 8 seed bead (left to right direction).

11. On each strand string: 3 size 11 seed beads.

12. On the right strand, string a crimp tube. Insert the left strand through the crimp tube and the size 11 seed bead next to the crimp tube on the right strand. Insert

the right strand through the size 11 seed bead to the left of the crimp tube. Pull the strands taut.

13. Crimp the crimp tube with chain-nose pliers, and trim the excess wire.

14. Attach the dangle to the ear wire.

15. Repeat steps 1–14 to complete the second earring.

DARK BLUISH GREEN CRYSACOLA RECTANGLES

Page 12   Length: 1½"

Instructions

String onto a head pin: 1 silver round, 1 spacer, 1 crysacola (chrysocolla) rectangle, 1 spacer, 1 silver round. Turn a plain loop on top, and then attach the dangle to the ear wire. Repeat to complete the second earring.

CAT'S-EYE STRIPES

Page 12   Length: 1"

Instructions

String onto a head pin: 1 bead cap, 1 lampworked bead, 1 bead cap, 1 silver round. Begin a wrapped loop on top. String the loop through the loop of an ear wire and complete the wrap. Repeat to complete the second earring.

KYANITE RECTANGLE WITH DANGLE

Page 13   Length: 2¼"

Instructions

1. Make a wrapped loop on one end of a piece of wire. String the large kyanite rectangle onto the wire and make a wrapped loop on top.

2. String onto a head pin: 1 small kyanite rectangle. Begin a wrapped loop on top.

3. String the loop through one loop on the large kyanite bead and complete the wrap. Attach the dangle to the ear wire.

4. Repeat steps 1–3 to complete the second earring.

KYANITE AND ICE

Page 13   Length: 1⅛"

Instructions

String onto a head pin: 1 kyanite square, 1 silver round, 1 rondelle, 1 silver round. Turn a plain loop on top, and then attach the dangle to the decorated post. Repeat to complete the second earring.

DREAMSICLE

Page 14   Length: 2⅜"

Instructions

1. String the following beads onto head pins and make a wrapped loop on the top of each.

   - 1 black-and-white round, 1 salmon pearl (2 units total)
   - 1 salmon pearl, 1 seed bead (2 units total)

2. Gently open a jump ring. String 1 photo anchor and the end link of one chain piece onto the jump ring and close the ring to secure.

3. Move up 4 links in the chain and attach a black-and-white dangle using a jump ring. Move up 3 more links in the chain and attach a seed bead dangle using a jump ring. Move up 2 more links in the chain and attach a photo anchor using a jump ring.

4. Feed the remaining chain through a lampworked disc. Attach the chain to the posie with a jump ring.

5. Attach the dangle to the ear wire.

6. Repeat steps 1–5 to complete the second earring.

ROSIE

Page 14   Length: 2¾"

Instructions

1. String the following beads onto head pins and make a wrapped loop on top of each.

   - 1 crystal bicone, 1 onyx round
   - 1 onyx round, 1 curved tube
   - 1 crystal bicone, 1 curved tube, 1 onyx round
   - 1 crystal bicone, 1 spiral tab, 1 onyx round

2. Gently open a 4 mm jump ring. String the 4 dangles and a 3 mm jump ring onto the open jump ring and close to secure.

3. Open an eye pin, attach the 3 mm jump ring and close the eye pin to secure.

4. String onto the eye pin: 1 sterling bicone, 1 Venetian tab, 1 sterling bicone. Make a wrapped loop on top.

5. Open an eye pin, attach the dangle, and close the eye pin to secure.

6. String onto the eye pin: 1 sterling bicone, 1 lampworked bead, 1 sterling bicone. Make a wrapped loop on top.

7. Attach the dangle to the ear wire.

8. Repeat steps 1–7 to complete the second earring.

BLACK ONYX RECTANGLES

Page 15   Length: 2⅛"

Instructions

1. String onto a head pin: 1 V-shaped bead, 1 silver diamond-shaped bead. Make a wrapped loop on top

2. Turn a plain loop at the end of one length of wire. Gently open the loop on the wire, string the "V" unit onto the loop, and close the loop to secure.

3. String the onyx rectangle onto the wire. Turn a plain loop on top.

4. Attach the dangle to the ear wire.

5. Repeat steps 1–4 to complete the second earring.

PINK COIN PEARLS

Page 15   Length: 1⅜"

Instructions

String onto a head pin: 1 coin pearl, 1 spacer, 1 silver round. Turn a plain loop. Gently open the plain loop, attach the ear wire, and close the loop to secure. Repeat to complete the second earring.

KIWI JASPER AND BLACK ONYX

Page 16   Length: 2⅞"

Instructions

1. String onto a head pin: 1 kiwi jasper square, 1 black coin, 1 spacer, 1 black coin. Turn a plain loop on top.

2. Turn a plain loop on one end of a length of wire. String onto the wire: 1 kiwi jasper square, 1 black coin, 1 spacer, 1 black coin. Turn a plain loop on top.

3. Gently open the loop at the bottom of the unit, string on the beaded head-pin unit, and close the loop to secure.

4. Attach the dangle to an ear wire.

5. String onto a head pin: 1 black coin, 1 spacer, 1 black coin, 1 kiwi jasper square. Turn a plain loop on top.

6. Turn a plain loop on one end of a length of wire. String onto the wire: 1 black coin, 1 spacer, 1 black coin, 1 kiwi jasper square. Turn a plain loop on top. Attach the dangle to an ear wire.

AMAZONITE RECTANGLES WITH BLACK ONYX DROPS

Page 16   Length: 2¾"

Instructions

1. Cut the wire into the following lengths:

   - 2 lengths, each 1⅝"
   - 2 lengths, each 1⅛"

2. String onto a head pin: 1 onyx round, 1 spacer, 1 onyx round, 1 spacer, 1 onyx round. Turn a plain loop on top.

3. Turn a plain loop on the end of a 1⅛" length of wire. Gently open the loop, attach the onyx unit, and close the loop.

4. String onto the wire stem: 1 flower bead, 1 silver round. Make a wrapped loop on top.

5. Turn a plain loop on the end of a 1⅝" length of wire. Open the loop, attach the flower unit, and close the loop.

6. String onto the wire stem: 1 amazonite rectangle, 2 spacers, 1 silver round. Make a wrapped loop on top.

7. Attach the dangle to the ear wire.

8. Repeat steps 2–7 to complete the second earring.

LARGE GREEN TURQUOISE BALLS
Page 17   Length: 2"

Instructions

String 1 turquoise bead onto a head pin. Begin a wrapped loop on top. String the loop onto the bottom loop of a connector and complete the wraps to secure. Attach the dangle to the ear wire. Repeat to complete the second earring.

GREEN RIBBED JADE
Page 17   Length: 1½"

Instructions

String onto a head pin: 1 large spacer, 1 jade bead, 1 small spacer, 3 fluorite rondelles. Turn a plain loop on top of the beads. Attach the dangle to the ear wire. Repeat to complete the second earring.

STERLING NOODLES AND SHIMMERING CRYSTALS
Page 18   Length: 1¾"

Instructions

1. String onto a length of flexible beading wire: 1 crimp tube, 1 spacer, an

alternating pattern of 5 small crystal bicones and 4 silver noodles, starting with a small crystal bicone, 1 spacer.

2. Insert the end of the flexible beading wire into the crimp tube, the daisy spacer and the crystal. Insert the other end of the wire through the daisy 1 spacer and crystal on the other side of the crimp.

3. Pull each end of the wire to tighten the beads, crimp the crimp tube with chain-nose pliers, and trim the excess wire.

4. String onto a head pin: 1 spacer, 1 large crystal bicone, 1 spacer, 1 small crystal bicone. Turn a plain loop on top.

5. Gently open a jump ring, string the crystal unit onto it, and close the jump ring to secure.

6. Open a second jump ring, attach it to the jump ring on the dangle and the center of the earring at the crimp, and close the jump ring to secure.

7. Open a third jump ring, attach it to the dangle and to the loop of an ear wire. Close the jump ring to secure.

8. Repeat steps 1–7 to complete the second earring.

FRESHWATER COIN PEARLS AND CRYSTALS
Page 18   Length: 1⅛"

Instructions

String onto a head pin: 1 freshwater pearl, 1 spacer, 1 crystal bicone. Make a wrapped loop on top, and then attach the dangle to the ear wire. Repeat to complete the second earring.

HAMMERED SILVER HOOPS
Page 19   Length: 1⅜"

Instructions

String onto a head pin: 1 silver oval. Begin a wrapped loop on top. String the loop through a jump ring and complete the wrap.

Attach the hammered circle and dangle to the ear wire. Repeat to complete the second earring.

SATURN MOONS
Page 19   Length: 1½"

Instructions

1. String onto a head pin: 1 potato pearl. Begin a wrapped loop on top.

2. String the loop through a hole in the silver circle link and complete the wrap.

3. String onto a head pin: 1 pearl coin. Make a wrapped loop on top. Attach the ear wire through the loop of the pearl coin and the remaining hole in the silver circle link.

4. Repeat steps 1–3 to complete the second earring.

RED LEATHER
Page 20   Length: 1⅞"

Instructions

1. String a leather bead onto a head pin. Use a dot of jeweler's cement to secure it, if necessary, so the pin will not slip through the bead. Make a wrapped loop on top.

2. Open a connector loop, attach the leather dangle, and close the loop to secure. Attach the ear wire to the top of the connector.

3. Repeat steps 1 and 2 to complete the second earring.

BROWN CARVED JASPER LANTERNS
Page 20   Length: 1¼"

Instructions

1. String onto a head pin: 1 jasper barrel, 1 spacer, 1 rondelle. If desired, use a dab of jeweler's cement at the bottom of the jasper barrel to keep the bead centered over the head pin.

2. Turn a plain loop on top, and then attach the dangle to the ear wire.

3. Repeat steps 1 and 2 to complete the second earring.

SQUARES AND SILVER
Page 21   Length: 1½"

Instructions

String onto a head pin: 1 Czech bead, 1 spacer, 1 chip, 1 melon bead. Turn a plain loop on top, and then attach the dangle to the ear wire. Repeat to complete the second earring.

CARNELIAN CARVED OVALS
Page 21   Length: 2⅛"

Instructions

1. String a head pin from the inside bottom of the oval ring through to the outside and make a wrapped loop.

2. Turn a loop at one end of a 1¼" length of wire. String a triangle, pointed end down, onto the wire and begin a wrapped loop on top. String the loop through the loop at the bottom of the oval ring and complete the wrap.

3. String a head pin from the inside top of the oval ring through to the outside. String onto the head pin: 1 spacer, 1 rondelle, 1 spacer.

4. Begin a wrapped loop on top. Insert the loop through the loop of the ear wire and complete the wrap.

5. Repeat steps 1–4 to complete the second earring.

IRIDESCENT SHELL DOUGHNUT WITH PEARL DANGLE
Page 22   Length: 2⅝"

Instructions

1. String a ball head pin from the inside bottom of the shell doughnut through to the outside and begin a wrapped loop.

2. String the loop through the top loop of a decorative link and complete the wrap.

3. String onto a ball head pin: 1 pearl, 1 spacer, 1 pearl, 1 spacer, 1 pearl. Begin a wrapped loop. String the loop through the bottom loop of the decorative link and complete the wrap.

4. String a plain head pin from the inside top of the shell doughnut through to the outside and begin a wrapped loop. String the loop through the loop of an ear wire and complete the wrap.

5. Repeat steps 1–4 to complete the second earring.

YELLOW AND BLUE TURQUOISE
Page 22   Length: 1½"

Instructions

String onto a head pin: 1 yellow turquoise coin, 1 spacer, 1 turquoise barrel, 1 spacer. Turn a plain loop on top, and then attach the dangle to the ear wire. Repeat to complete the second earring.

PAUA OVALS
Page 23   Length: 1⅝"

Instructions

String onto a head pin: 1 bicone, 1 Paua shell oval, 1 bicone. Make a wrapped loop on top, and then attach the dangle to the ear wire. Repeat to complete the second earring.

TWO RINGS WITH DANGLE
Page 23   Length: 1¾"

Instructions

1. String onto a head pin: 1 labradorite bead, 1 apatite rondelle, 1 peridot rondelle, 1 apatite rondelle, 1 labradorite bead. Turn a plain loop.

2. Gently open the loop on top of the beads. String the dangle onto a large silver ring and close the loop.

3. Open the jump ring and string on the large silver ring of the dangle and the loop of an ear wire. Close the jump ring.

4. Repeat steps 1–3 to complete the second earring.

CONTEMPO CHARM
Page 24   Length: 2⅝"

Instructions

1. String onto a head pin: one pewter swirl, one 4 mm bicone, one seed bead. Begin a wrapped loop on top.

2. String the loop through the last link of a piece of 2 mm chain and complete the wrap to secure.

3. String the beads as listed below onto head pins and begin a wrapped loop on top of each. Attach the dangles to the 4 mm chain, alternating the placement on the left and right sides of the chain, and complete the wraps in the following order from the bottom link of the chain (link A) up to link F.

Link A: One 5 mm bicone, one spacer, one 3 mm charteuse facetted round.

Link B: One 5 mm round, one seed bead

Link C: One chartreuse rough-cut, one 2 mm silver round.

Link D: 1 pink round, 1 (E) bead, 1 pink round

Link E: One 4 mm bicone, one spacer, one 4 mm bicone, one seed bead

Link F: one faceted doughnut, one 4 mm saucer, one 2 mm silver round

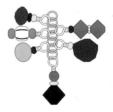

4. String onto a head pin: 1 cube, 1 seed bead. Make a wrapped loop on top of the beads. *Do not* attach this one to the chain.

5. Begin a wrapped loop on one end of a piece of wire. String the chain dangle, the pewter swirl chain dangle, and the cube dangle onto the loop, and complete the wraps to secure.

6. String onto the wire: one angel wing, one anodized aluminum barrel, one 8 mm saucer, one 3 mm silver round. Make a wrapped loop on the top.

7. Attach the dangle to the ear wire.

8. Repeat steps 1–7 to complete the second earring.

ON A ROLL

Page 24 **Length:** 2"

Instructions

1. String onto a head pin: 1 beehive, 1 sterling silver disk, 1 bicone, 1 silver round. Make a wrapped loop on top.

2. Gently open the loop on an eye pin, string the beehive dangle onto the eye pin, and close the loop to secure.

3. String onto eye pin: 1 die, 1 Czech round. Make a wrapped loop on top, and then attach the dangle to the ear wire.

4. Repeat steps 1–3 to complete the second earring.

CONICAL SWIRL

Page 25 **Length:** 1½"

Instructions

1. Straighten the wire as much as possible. Make a tight wire coil, stopping about 1" from the end.

2. Make a small loop on the end of the wire, turning the loop away from the coil.

3. Press slowly on the center of the coil using the eraser end of a pencil to spread the coils out to create a cone shape. Keep working each coil apart with an even gap between each one.

4. Grasp the wire ⅜" from the end of the small loop with round-nose pliers and roll the pliers to rotate the small loop to the center bottom of the cone. Make any

adjustments to the wire as necessary so the loop at the top of the cone aligns with the loop at the bottom of the cone.

5. String onto a head pin: 1 clear round, 1 wire cone, 1 black round. Make a wrapped loop on top, and then attach the dangle to the ear wire.

6. Repeat steps 1–5 to complete the second earring.

DANCING DISC

Page 25 **Length:** 1⅞"

Instructions

1. String onto a head pin: 1 bicone, 1 zigzag bead, 1 bicone of a different color. Make a wrapped loop on top of the beads.

2. Gently open the loop on the eye pin, attach the zigzag dangle, and close the loop to secure.

3. String onto an eye pin: 1 lampworked disc, 1 spacer, 1 silver round. Make a wrapped loop on top, and then attach the dangle to the ear wire.

4. Repeat steps 1–3, reversing the bicone colors on the zigzag dangle to complete the second earring.

LOTUS BLOSSOMS

Page 26 **Length:** 1½"

Instructions

1. String onto a head pin: 1 daisy bead cap, 1 filigree bead cap, 1 jadeite round (gently form the filigree bead cap with hands around the jadeite bead), 2 closed jump rings, 1 fluorite round. Turn a plain loop on top.

2. Gently open a jump ring, string through the loop of the dangle and the loop of an ear wire, and close the jump ring to secure.

3. Repeat steps 1 and 2 to complete the second earring.

ETERNITY BUTTERFLY GARDENS

Page 26 **Length:** 1⅞"

Instructions

1. String onto an eye pin: one 4 mm Satin Smoked Topaz crystal, 1 glass doughnut, one 4 mm Satin Smoked Topaz crystal. Turn a plain loop on top.

2. String the following beads onto head pins and make a wrapped loop on the top of each.

   • one 3 mm Smoked Topaz crystal (2 units total)

   • 1 Lime crystal

   • 1 Pacific Opal crystal

3. Gently open one end of the eye pin containing the glass doughnut and crystals. String a 3 mm crystal drop onto the loop and close the loop to secure.

4. Gently open a 5.25 mm jump ring. String the Lime crystal drop onto the jump ring, attach the jump ring through the eternity garden ring and the eye pin of the doughnut bead link containing the 3 mm crystal drop, and close the jump ring to secure.

5. Gently open a 4.75 mm jump ring. String the second 3 mm Smoked Topaz crystal drop and the Pacific Opal drop onto the jump ring. Slide the jump ring through the loop of the filigree butterfly charm and through another 4.75 mm jump ring and close to secure.

6. Attach the second 4.75 mm jump ring at the top of the butterfly cluster to the 5.25 mm jump ring that is attached to the eternity garden ring and close to secure.

7. Gently open a 5.25 mm jump ring and string it through the dangle and the ear wire. Close the jump ring.

8. Repeat steps 1–7 to complete the second earring.

RING AROUND THE PERFECT PEARL
Page 27   Length: 1½"

Instructions

1. String onto a head pin: 1 pearl, 1 bead cap (gently form the filigree bead cap with hands around the pearl). Make a wrapped loop on top.

2. Gently open a 4.75 mm jump ring. Attach the pearl drop and close the jump ring to secure.

3. Gently open another 4.75 jump ring. String a hammered ring and the pearl unit onto the jump ring and close to secure.

4. Gently open an etched jump ring. String the hammered ring-and-pearl unit and an ear wire onto the jump ring and close to secure.

5. Repeat steps 1–4 to complete the second earring.

FIRE AND ICE
Page 27   Length: 2¾"

Instructions

1. String the following beads onto a head pin and turn a plain loop on top.
   - 1 Fire Opal crystal (2 units total)
   - 1 turquoise crystal

2. String onto the center of an eye pin: 1 crystal faceted drop. Bring both ends of the eye pin up toward the top of the crystal, with the loop of the eye pin slightly above the crystal and crossing the wires to form an X. Complete a wire-wrapped bail, referring to "Basics" on page 59. Use the looped end of the wire as the vertical wire.

3. Gently open a jump ring, string it through the loop of a Turquoise crystal drop and through an opening at the center bottom of a crest filigree, and close the jump ring to secure.

4. Gently open a jump ring, string it through the loop of a Fire Opal crystal and through an opening on the center right of the crest filigree, and then close the jump ring to secure. Repeat this step on the center left of the crest filigree.

5. Gently open the loop on an ear wire, string it through the center top of the crest filigree and through the crystal faceted drop, and then close the loop to secure.

6. Repeat steps 1–5 to complete the second earring.

STONES AND DIAMONDS
Page 28   Length: 1⅞"

Instructions

1. Center a ceramic pendant on one length of wire. Bend each wire end upward, crossing them to form an X.

2. Position one of the wires straight up over the center top of the pendant and bend the other wire horizontally so it is perpendicular to the first wire.

3. Wrap the horizontal wire a couple of times around the vertical wire and trim the excess.

4. String onto the pendant wire: 1 chip, 1 seed bead, 1 chip. Make a wrapped loop on top, and then attach the dangle to an ear wire.

5. Repeat steps 1–4 to complete the second earring.

GOLDEN PEARLS AND CLAY
Page 28   Length: 1⅞"

Instructions

Follow steps 1–3 for "Stones and Diamonds" above. String onto the pendant wire: 1 seed bead, 1 pearl, 1 seed bead. Make a wrapped loop on top, and then attach the dangle to the ear wire. Repeat to complete the second earring.

CORAL SPIRAL CHANDELIERS
Page 29   Length: 3"

Instructions

1. Cut the gold-filled wire into 4 equal lengths.

2. Wrap the end of one of the gold-filled wires at least 3 times around the top of the longest spiral, next to the top loop, being sure to wrap tightly.

3. String a bead onto the wire, hold the bead against the spiral frame, secure with 3 or more wraps around the frame below the bead.

4. Repeat step 3 using the different beads from your materials list, saving 6 coral chips, 2 Siam 8 mm Swarovski crystal domed spacers, two 4.5 mm Swarovksi crystal bicones, and 2 gold daisy spacers for the drops on the bottom of each spiral.

5. End with 3 or more wraps around the spiral frame, above the bottom loop of the frame.

6. Repeat steps 2–5 for the shorter spiral.

7. String onto a head pin: 1 Crystal Brandy bicone, 1 Siam domed spacer, 1 daisy spacer. Begin a wrapped loop. String the loop through the loop at the bottom of the short spiral and complete the wrap.

8. String 3 coral chips onto a head pin and begin a wrapped loop on top. String the loop through the loop at the bottom of the long spiral and complete the wrap.

9. Attach the beaded finding to the earring post.

10. Repeat steps 2–9 to complete the second earring.

GOLDEN AUTUMN

Page 29   Length: 2⅛"

Instructions

1. Starting on the upper-right side of a gold leaf, wrap one end of a piece of 28-gauge wire around an opening in the filigree (avoiding the outer edge of the leaf) 3 times to secure, ending up on the front side. Tuck the cut end of the wire into the filigree.

2. String 1 crystal bicone onto the wire sliding it up close to the leaf.

3. String the wire back down through the leaf and bring it back up to the front of the leaf through a different hole. String the wire through random holes in the leaf, determined by how you would like the crystals to lie. The goal is to travel along the outer edge of the leaf keeping the outer edge free of wire. The crystals do not need to lie in a straight row; irregular placement lends to a natural look. Keep the wire as smooth and straight as possible to avoid breakage.

4. Repeat steps 2 and 3 to attach additional crystal bicones, until the bottom point of the leaf is reached.

5. Cut the chain in half. You will need 2 sets of 3 links each.

6. Secure one chain length to the bottom of the leaf by threading your wire through one end link. Wrap the wire around the outside of the leaf and back up through the filigree to secure, making sure the chain hangs straight down.

7. Continue adding crystals along the left side of the leaf and bind off by wrapping the wire 3 times around an opening in the filigree.

8. String 1 crystal bicone each onto 5 head pins and begin wrapped loops on top of each.

9. String a head pin loop through the bottom link of the chain and complete the wrap to secure.

10. Follow step 9 to secure 2 crystal bicones to each of the remaining links in the chain, attaching 1 bicone to each side of each link.

11. Begin a wrapped loop at one end of a piece of 24-gauge wire. String the wire through the top loop of the leaf and complete the wrap.

12. String a crystal bicone onto the wire, and make a wrapped loop on top, and then attach the beaded finding to the ear wire.

13. Repeat steps 1–12 to complete the second earring.

AMBER, JET, AND CORAL DROPS

Page 30   Length: 2⅛"

Instructions

1. On a 2½" piece of wire, measure 1" from one end. Using needle-nose pliers, bend the short end up to form a 45° angle. String a coral teardrop onto the other end of the wire. Measure 1" from the other end of the wire and bend that side up to form a 45° angle. The wires should cross one another forming an X above the bead. Complete the wire-wrapped bail, turning a plain loop on top.

2. Turn a plain loop on one end of a short piece of wire. String onto the wire: 1 jet rondelle, 1 amber square, 1 jet rondelle. Turn a plain loop on top.

3. Open the loop at the bottom of the jet rondelle, attach the coral unit, and close the loop. Attach the dangle to the ear wire.

4. Repeat steps 1–3 to complete the second earring.

BIRDS WITH GARNET

Page 30   Length: 1⅞"

Instructions

1. String onto a head pin: 1 garnet diamond, 1 small spacer, 1 garnet round. Turn a plain loop on top.

2. Turn a plain loop at one end of a piece of wire. Gently open the loop, attach the garnet dangle, and close the loop.

3. String onto the wire: 1 ceramic coin, 1 Saturn-shaped spacer, 1 silver round. Begin a wrapped loop on top. String the loop through the loop of an ear wire and complete the wrap.

4. Repeat steps 1–3 to complete the second earring.

LABRADORITE DOUGHNUTS WITH GARNET CLUSTER

Page 31   Length: 2⅜"

Instructions

1. On a 2¾" piece of wire, measure 1⅛" from one end. Using needle nose pliers, bend the short end up to form a 45° angle. String a garnet cluster onto the other end of the wire. Measure ¾" from the other end of the wire, and bend that side up to form a 45° angle. The wires should cross one another forming an X above the bead. Complete the wire-wrapped bail, making a wrapped loop on top.

2. String onto a ball head pin: 1 garnet round, 1 spacer. String the end of the head pin from the inside top of the doughnut bead through to the outside, and make a wrapped loop on top.

3. Insert a plain head pin from the inside bottom of the doughnut through to the outside. Begin a wrapped loop. String the loop through the loop of the garnet drop and complete the wrap.

4. Attach the dangle to the ear wire.

5. Repeat steps 1–4 to complete the second earring.

SILVER COINS WITH BRONZE PEARL AND GARNET DROPS

Page 31   Length: 1⅞"

Instructions

1. String onto a head pin: 1 garnet round, 1 spacer, 1 pearl, 1 spacer, 1 garnet round. Turn a plain loop on top.

2. Turn a plain loop on one end of a piece of wire. String onto the wire: 1 silver coin. Begin a wrapped loop on top. String the loop onto an ear wire loop and complete the wrap.

3. Gently open the loop at the top of the garnet dangle, string onto the loop at the bottom of the silver coin, and close the loop to secure.

4. Repeat steps 1–3 to complete the second earring.

CHAIN MAIL

Page 32   Length: 1½"

Instructions

1. Gently open a 10 mm jump ring. String the jump ring through the lampworked bead and close to secure.

2. Open two 7 mm jump rings, attach both to the 10 mm jump ring, and close.

3. Open two 5 mm jump rings, string onto both 7 mm jump rings, and close.

4. Open a 3.5 mm jump ring, string onto both 5 mm jump rings and an ear wire, and close to secure.

5. Repeat steps 1–4 to complete the second earring.

GREEN TOURMALINE FRINGE

Page 32   Length: 1⅜"

Instructions

1. String a tourmaline round onto a head pin and begin a wrapped loop on top. String the loop through one of the bottom openings of the filigree teardrop and complete the wrap.

2. Repeat step 1 to attach a total of 7 beads to the lower edge of the filigree teardrop. Attach the dangle to the ear wire.

3. Repeat steps 1 and 2 to complete the second earring.

PINK TOURMALINE FRINGE

Page 33   Length: 1⅜"

Instructions

1. String a tourmaline round onto a head pin and begin a wrapped loop on top. String the loop through the center bottom opening on the filigree finding and complete the wrap.

2. Repeat step 1 for a total of 11 more tourmaline rounds, attaching 10 more beads evenly on either side of the center bead. Attach the final bead to the top inside loop of the filigree finding.

3. Attach the dangle to the ear wire.

4. Repeat steps 1–3 to complete the second earring.

PURPLE LAMPWORKED BEADS

Page 33   Length: 1⅜"

Instructions

1. String onto a 24-gauge eye pin: 1 tourmaline rondelle, 1 silver spacer, 1 lampworked bead, 1 silver spacer. Begin a wrapped loop on top.

2. Cut a 2-link section of chain. String the partially wrapped end of the eye pin through an end link and complete the wrap to secure.

3. String 1 tourmaline rondelle onto each of seven 26-gauge eye pins and begin a wrapped loop on top of each.

4. String a loop on a tourmaline dangle through the bottom chain link and complete the wrap to secure. Repeat two more times, placing a dangle on each side of the first one.

5. Attach a dangle to each side of the top chain link in the same manner. Attach a dangle to each side of the wrapped loop above the chain links. Attach the dangle to the ear wire.

6. Repeat steps 1–5 to complete the second earring.

BASKETWEAVE

Page 34   Length: 2⅛"

Instructions

1. Cut 18-gauge wire into the following lengths, flush cutting the wire on both ends:
   - 4 lengths, each 2½"
   - 2 lengths, each 1⅛"

2. Using round-nose pliers, make a loop in one end of a 2½" piece of wire as for making a loose wire coil. Continue coiling the wire to make a loose, open circle around the loop.

3. Make a loop on the other end of the wire, rolling the wire in the opposite direction. Continue to coil the wire loosely halfway around the loop. Shape the wire as necessary to create an S as shown.

4. Repeat steps 2 and 3 to make a second S-shaped wire piece. Be sure that the shaped wire pieces are the same height. Adjust as necessary. Turn one piece over to make a reverse S. The two pieces should be mirror image.

5. Place the shaped wire pieces on a bench block, cushioned with a pounding pad, and pound with a chasing hammer. Pound with the face on the outside of the curves to emphasize the form and strengthen.

6. Distress the front of each piece by hitting with the ball peen side of the chasing hammer.

7. Position the S shapes together to create a symmetrical design as shown. Wrap the 24-gauge wire around the top of one of the S shapes, just below where they nearly touch, carrying the wire across the left half from left to right. Thread the wire between the two sides, under the right half of the design, over the top, then down through the shapes at the middle. Wrap under the left side, over the top, through the middle, under the right side, and over the top. Continue the over and under weaving for about 5 or 6 wraps to secure the pieces together at the top.

8. Repeat the weaving at the bottom of the design to join the bottom halves, starting under the wire loops and weaving toward the outside. Leave a 1" tail.

9. Wrap the wire ends twice around one side of the wire frame and trim the ends on the back.

10. Place the round-nose pliers in the center of a 1 1/8" length of wire. Pull on both ends of the wires with the other hand to create an inverted V.

11. Using the round-nose pliers, roll the wire in from each end to create matching loops.

12. Pound the top of the inverted V and the bottom of the loops with a chasing hammer. Distress with the ball peen hammer.

13. Gently open a jump ring and attach the left loop of the inverted V and the left loop of the S frame. Close the jump ring. Repeat on the right side.

14. Open a jump ring, connect to the bottom of the S frame on the left side, and close. Repeat on the right side.

15. String a pearl onto each of three head pins. Make a wrapped loop on top.

16. Open a jump ring; string it through the bottom two jump rings of the S frame and through the loops on the pearl dangles. Close the jump ring to secure.

17. Open the loop at the bottom of an ear wire, string on the inverted V so the ends of the weaving wires are at the back of the earring, and close the loop to secure.

18. Repeat steps 2–17 to complete the second earring.

19. Add a patina finish to the earrings if desired using liver of sulfur and following the manufacturer's directions.

SPIRALS
Page 34   Length: 1"
Instructions
1. Using round-nose pliers, make a loop on one end of a 2½" piece of wire as for making a wire coil. Continue coiling the wire to make a loose, open coil around the loop.

2. Make a loop on the other end of the wire, rolling the wire in the opposite direction. Continue to coil the wire loosely halfway around the loop. Shape the wire as necessary to create an S, with the top and bottom coils on top of each other and nearly touching as shown.

3. Repeat steps 1 and 2 to make a second S-shaped wire piece. Turn one piece over to make a reverse S.

4. Place the shaped wire pieces on a bench block, cushioned with a pounding pad, and pound with a chasing hammer. Pound with the face on the outside of the curves to emphasize the form and strengthen.

5. Distress the front of each piece by hitting with the ball peen side of the chasing hammer.

6. Wrap the 24-gauge wire around the bottom coil near the loop, where the top and bottom coils nearly touch (refer to the project photo on page 34). Carry the wire across the front of the wire frame from bottom to top. Thread the wire between the top and bottom coils, under the wire of the top coil, over the top, then down between the top and bottom coils, under the wire of the bottom coil, over the bottom, and then down between the top and bottom coils. Continue the over-and-under weaving for about 5 or 6 wraps to secure the pieces together.

7. Wrap the wire ends twice around the wire of the S frame, and trim the ends on the back. Attach the S to the ear wire.

8. Repeat steps 1–7 to complete the second earring.

9. Add a patina finish to the earrings if desired using liver of sulfur and following the manufacturer's directions.

LOOP DE LOOP VINES
Page 35   Length: 2"
Instructions
1. Starting in the center of the round-nose pliers' jaws, make a loop in one end of a piece of wire as for starting a tight wire coil.

2. Hold the loop just completed with your nondominant hand from underneath, with the loop rolled facing toward you. This allows you to work away from yourself giving you leverage. Move the pliers about 1/2" down the wire. Grab the wire near the tip of the pliers and roll your hand away and make the next loop. Reposition your piece and hold the circle just completed from underneath.

3. Repeat step 2 two more times to make two more loops, but keep loops 2, 3, and 4, close together and make loop 3 larger.

4. Make the final loop at the end of the wire. It should be about 1/2" away from the last loop formed.

5. Place the shaped wire pieces on a bench block, cushioned with a pounding pad, and pound gently on the outside of each circle with the chasing hammer, taking care not to pound too hard where the wires cross.

6. String 1 crystal bicone, 1 pearl, and 1 faceted pearl with a bead cap each onto separate head pins and begin a wrapped loop on top of each.

7. String 1 of the loops through one of the lower 3 loops of the wire loop de loop frame, referring to the project photo for placement, and complete the wrap to secure. Repeat for the remaining beaded head pins.

8. Attach the dangle to the ear wire.

9. Repeat steps 1–8 to complete the second earring.

10. Add a patina finish to the earrings if desired using liver of sulfur and following the manufacturer's directions.

LOOP DE LOOP SUNRAYS
Page 35 Length: 2 1/8"

Instructions

1. Cut 18-gauge wire into the following lengths, flush cutting the wire on both ends:

- 2 lengths, each 6"
- 2 lengths, each 1 1/8"

2. Using round-nose pliers, make a loop on one end of a 6" piece of wire, as for making a tight wire coil.

3. Holding the loop facing up and toward you, make 6 more loops, starting each about 1/8" away from the previous loop and rolling the pliers away from you; increase the size of each of the next three loops. Decrease the size of each of the next three loops, so they match the size of the first three loops in reverse order. You should have a straight line of loops all on the same side of the wire.

4. Shape the wire into a circular shape using chain-nose pliers as necessary. The two smallest loops should touch at the center top, but not overlap.

5. Place the shaped wire pieces on a bench block, cushioned with a pounding pad, and pound gently on the outside of each circle with the chasing hammer, taking care not to pound too hard where the wires cross.

6. Place the round-nose pliers in the center of a 1 1/8" length of wire. Pull on both ends of the wires with the other hand to create an inverted V.

7. Using the round-nose pliers, roll the wire in from each end to create matching loops.

8. Pound the top of the inverted V and the bottom of the loops with a chasing hammer.

9. Gently open a jump ring and attach the left loop of the inverted V and the left loop of the wire frame. Close the jump ring. Repeat on the right side.

10. String the following beads onto separate head pins and begin a wrapped loop on top of each.

- 1 crystal bicone (2 units total)
- One 4 mm pearl (2 units total)
- One 10 mm pearl, 1 bead cap

11. String the head pin with the 10 mm pearl through the bottom center loop of the wire frame and complete the wrap to secure.

12. String a head pin with a 4 mm pearl through the right bottom loop of the wire frame and complete the wrap. Repeat for a crystal bicone.

13. Repeat step 12 on the left bottom loop of the wire frame.

14. Open the loop at the bottom of an ear wire, string on the inverted V, and close the loop to secure.

15. Repeat steps 2–14 to complete the second earring.

16. Add a patina finish to the earrings if desired using liver of sulfur and following the manufacturer's directions.

SILVER DOTS
Page 36 Length: 1"

Instructions

1. String onto a head pin: 1 metallic coin, 1 spacer, 1 silver round. Turn a plain loop on top, and then attach the dangle to the ear wire. Repeat to complete the second earring.

PURPLE AND SAGE RECTANGLES WITH SPIRAL FINDINGS

Page 36   Length: 1¾"

Instructions

String onto a head pin: 1 stone rectangle, 1 spacer, 1 rondelle, 1 silver round. Turn a plain loop on top, and then attach the dangle to the ear wire. Repeat to complete the second earring.

BUTTERFLIES

Page 37   Length: 1⅞"

Instructions

1. Cut chain into 2 sections of 7 links each.

2. Gently open the loop on the ear wire. String the last link on one end of a chain onto the ear wire and close the loop to secure.

3. String the following beads onto head pins and begin a wrapped loop on top of each.

    • 1 Maroon pearl (2 units total)

    • 1 Golden Shadow bicone (2 units total)

    • 1 black faceted round (2 units total)

4. String the loop of each beaded head pin through a link in the chain, starting with the link the ear wire is attached to and following the order listed in step 3 twice, and then complete the wraps.

5. String onto a head pin: 1 gold-filled round, 1 butterfly bead. Begin a wrapped loop on top. String the loop through the last link of the chain and complete the wrap.

6. Repeat steps 2–5 to complete the second earring.

CHAROITE NUGGETS

Page 37   Length: 2¼"

Instructions

1. Begin a wrapped loop on the end of one length of wire.

2. String onto the wire: 1 silver round, 1 spacer, 1 nugget, 1 spacer, 1 silver round. Begin a wrapped loop, being sure to leave enough space on each end for the wraps.

3. String the loop onto the last link of one piece of chain and complete the wrap. Repeat on the other side. Be sure to wrap around all the exposed wire to prevent the beads from shifting.

4. Gently open a jump ring. String the last link of each chain and the ear wire onto the ring and close the ring to secure.

5. Repeat steps 1–4 to complete the second earring.

BLUEBIRDS

Page 38   Length: 2⅛"

Instructions

1. Gently open a jump ring. String the ring through the loop of a bird and the bottom two dangles of the chain (they will be even if you cut them that way). Close the jump ring.

2. String a rondelle onto a head pin. Begin a wrapped loop on top. String the loop through a ring dangle on the lower portion of the chain and complete the wrap to secure.

3. Repeat step 2 to attach a total of 7 rondelles to the chain, concentrating them near the lower half of the chain and toward the front.

4. Gently open the top dangle on the chain and string through the bottom loop of an ear wire. Close the dangle loop to secure.

5. Repeat steps 1–4 to complete the second earring.

ENAMEL CONES

Page 38   Length: 3⅝"

Instructions

1. Cut chain to the following lengths:

    • 2 lengths, each 15 links long

    • 2 lengths, each 13 links long

    • 2 lengths, each 11 links long

    • 2 lengths, each 9 links long

2. Separate the lengths of chain into two groups, each containing one of each length of chain.

3. Cut wire to the following lengths:

    • 8 lengths, each 2" long

    • 2 lengths, each 4" long

4. Make a wrapped loop on one end of a 2" length of wire. String onto the wire: an alternating pattern of three white Opal AB bicones and two cubes beginning with a bicone. Begin a wrapped loop on top. Repeat three more times.

5. String the loop end of a beaded wire through the last link of a piece of chain and complete the wrap to secure. Repeat with the remaining 3 lengths of beaded wire.

6. String one Crystal AB bicone onto a head pin. Turn a plain loop on top. Repeat 3 more times.

7. Gently open the plain loop on a Crystal AB unit, string onto the loop at the end of a beaded chain, and close the loop to secure. Repeat with the remaining Crystal AB units.

8. Begin a wrapped loop on the end of a 4" length of wire, making the loop approximately 1 mm smaller than the cone's wide end.

9. String the end link of the longest chain unit onto the wire. String the remaining chain segments onto the wire, stringing them on from longest to shortest. Complete the wrap to secure.

10. String the cone onto the wire over the wrapped loop. String onto the wire: one 4 mm silver round, one 2 mm silver round. Make a wrapped loop on top.

11. Attach the dangle to the ear wire

12. Repeat steps 4–11 to complete the second earring.

FULL MOON THROUGH BRANCHES

Page 39   Length: 2¼"

Instructions

1. String onto a head pin: 1 silver round, 1 coin pearl, 1 silver round. Begin a wrapped loop on top. String the loop through the bottom hole in the twig link, so it faces forward, and complete the wrap to secure.

2. String onto a head pin: 1 silver round, 1 pearl, 1 silver round. Begin a wrapped loop on top. String the loop through the loop of a chaton (the front side of the chaton is slightly flatter) and complete the wrap.

3. Repeat step 2 to make 3 more chaton-and-pearl dangles.

4. Gently open a jump ring and string it through a dangle and a hole in the twig link, so the dangle faces front. Close the jump ring to secure. Repeat to attach the remaining dangles to the twig link.

5. Carefully unroll the loop on the back of the ear wire a tiny bit and hook the twig onto it, so it faces front (the twig has a ".925" mark on the back, which you don't want to display). Reroll the loop.

6. Repeat steps 1–5 to complete the second earring.

VICTORIANA

Page 39   Length: 2⅜"

Instructions

1. String onto a head pin: 1 crystal, 1 silver-and-marcasite bead, 1 crystal. Begin a generous-sized wrapped loop

on top. String the loop through a silver twisted link and complete the wrap, making sure the narrow edge of the twisted link and front of the head pin are both facing forward (the twisted link *should not* look like an "O" when viewed from the front).

2. Gently open a 6 mm sterling Snapeez jump ring, string through the twisted link and the bottom loop of a hoop, and close to secure.

3. Repeat steps 1 and 2 for the second earring.

SLANTED DOORS

Page 40   Length: 2¼"

Instructions

1. Cut chain into four ⅝" lengths. Cut wire into four 1½" lengths.

2. String a carnelian rondelle onto a head pin and make a wrapped loop on top.

3. Make a wrapped loop on one end of a length of wire. String a silver patterned square onto the wire and begin a wrapped loop on top. Set aside.

4. String a piece of chain through the loop of a carnelian bead and wrap the chain (with bead attached) around a diagonal corner of a 16 mm square link. Adjust the length of the chain by removing links as necessary for a snug fit. String the end links of the chain onto the partially completed loop on the patterned square from step 3 and complete the loop.

5. Make a wrapped loop on the end of a piece of wire. String a carnelian bead onto the wire and begin a wrapped loop. Set aside.

6. String the loop on the top of the silver patterned square onto a length of chain, and wrap the chain around a diagonal corner of a 20 mm square link. Adjust the length of the chain by removing links as necessary for a snug fit. String the end links of the chain onto the partially

completed loop on the carnelian bead from step 5 and complete the wrap to secure.

7. Carefully unroll the loop on the back of the ear wire a tiny bit and hook the dangle onto it, so it faces front. Reroll the loop.

8. Repeat steps 2–7 to complete the second earring.

HORSESHOE NAIL DANGLES

Page 40   Length: 2¼"

Instructions

1. Glue 2 of the 1.76" horseshoe nails, flat sides together.

2. Glue 1 of the 1.95" horseshoe nails to either side of the 1.76" horseshoe unit, being sure to apply glue to the flat sides of the nails; position the nail just above the nail heads of the previously glued pair as shown in the project photo on page 40. Glue the remaining 1.95" horseshoe nail to the opposite side of the unit. Let dry.

3. Bend one piece of wire ¼" from the end to make a 45° angle.

4. Lay the bent end of the wire flat against the glued unit ½" down from the pointed ends of the nails. The end of the bent wire should be pointing toward the nail heads.

5. Holding the wire in place, start wrapping tightly around the nails, wrapping over the cut end of the wire, and laying each wrap close to the previous wrap. Stop just above the nail heads, making sure to end on the same side where you started; this will be the back of your earring.

6. Trim off the excess wire, leaving a ¼" tail. Use chain-nose pliers to tuck the tail up under the wrapped wire.

7. Place a little glue on the beginning and ending of the wire wrap.

8. Using chain-nose pliers, take a firm grip on the pointed tip of one of the outer nails, curl into a loop away from the main body of the earring. Repeat on the other side, making the loops even.

9. Gently open one 4 x 6 mm jump ring, string through one of the nail loops, and close the ring to secure.

10. Join five 3 x 4 mm jump rings together to make a chain. Open the end jump ring and attach to the 4 x 6 mm jump ring secured to the nail loop.

11. Open another 4 x 6 mm jump ring; string it through the last link of the jump ring chain and through the nail loop. Close to secure.

12. Open the loop at the bottom of an ear wire. String through the center jump ring of the chain, and close the loop to secure.

13. Repeat steps 1–13 to complete the second earring.

ORANGE BALL AND CRYSTALS
Page 41   Length: 1⅜"

Instructions

1. String onto a head pin: 1 spacer, 1 orange round, 1 spacer. Make a wrapped loop on top.

2. Gently open the loop on an ear wire, string through the loop in the orange dangle and through a silver ring. Close the loop to secure.

3. String a crystal bicone onto a head pin and begin a wrapped loop on top. String the silver ring through the loop and complete the wrap. Repeat two more times.

4. Repeat steps 1–3 to complete the second earring.

GREEN NUGGETS
Page 41   Length: 1⅛"

Instructions

1. Begin a wrapped loop at the end of a piece of wire. String a silver ring through the loop and complete the wrap.

2. String onto the wire: 1 rondelle, 1 nugget, 1 rondelle. Begin a wrapped loop on top.

3 Carry the strung beads across the ring and complete the wrap, securing the ring in the loop.

4. Gently open the loop on an ear wire, string through a wrapped loop of the strung beads, and close to secure.

5. Repeat steps 1–4 to complete the second earring.

CHAIN AND BEADS
Page 42   Length: 2⅝"

Instructions

1. String one 4–5 mm bead onto each of six head pins and make a wrapped loop at the top of each. Set aside.

2. Make a small wrapped loop on one end of a piece of wire. Slide a 6–8 mm bead down to the loop. Begin a wrapped loop on top, string the loop through 3 wrapped beads, an end loop of the chain, 3 more wrapped beads, and then complete the wraps to secure.

3. String a 4–5 mm bead onto a head pin and begin a wrapped loop. String the loop through a loop on one side of the chain, just below the previously attached beads and complete the wraps to secure. Repeat to add two more beads to the same loop, placing one on each side of the chain. Add three beads to the next loop in the chain in the same manner, alternating the placement of the single bead and the pair of beads.

4. Add a single bead to the bottom loop of the chain and continue wrapping the wire end of the head pin so it creates a coil on the top of the bead.

5. Attach the dangle to the ear wire.

6. Repeat steps 1–5 to complete the second earring.

7. Add a patina finish to the earrings if desired using liver of sulfur and following the manufacturer's directions.

BEAD WITH CLUSTER ON TOP
Page 42   Length: 1⅜"

Instructions

1. String a small bead onto each 1" head pin and make a wrapped loop on top.

2. String a silver square onto a 2½" head pin, then string a group of 12 smaller beads onto the head pin, stringing them in order from largest to smallest.

3. Make a wrapped loop on top of the group of beads, wrapping the wire around until the beads fit snug.

4. Attach the dangle to the ear wire.

5. Repeat steps 2–4 to complete the second earring.

6. Add a patina finish to the earrings if desired using liver of sulfur and following the manufacturer's directions.

WIRE FRAME WITH A SPIRAL
Page 43   Length: 2⅜"

Instructions

1. Using the flat nose pliers, fold one of the wire lengths over, 3" from the end.

2. Fold the wire over at a right angle, 1" from the same end, so the wire passes behind the other end of the wire as shown.

3. Make a slight angle in the longer end of the wire where the shorter wire end crosses it. Shape the wire as necessary so the two angles meet and the longer wire extends vertically above a narrow teardrop-shaped loop as shown.

4. Wrap the shorter end of the wire around the longer wire one complete wrap. Turn a plain loop at the end of the short wire. The loop should sit inside the oval wire frame, near the top. Make any necessary adjustments.

5. Make a wrapped loop in the long wire that sits on top of the oval wire frame; do not trim excess.

6. Make a flat coil on the end of the wire.

7. Place the shaped wire on a bench block, cushioned with a pounding pad, and pound the coil with the chasing hammer. Fold the coil over onto the oval wire frame. Using the chasing hammer, flatten the oval frame and top loop.

8. String onto a head pin: 1 spacer, 1 pearl. Make a wrapped loop on top

9. Gently open a jump ring and string it through the pearl dangle and the small loop in the top of the oval frame. Close the jump ring. Attach the dangle to the ear wire.

10. Repeat steps 1–9 to complete the second earring.

11. Add a patina finish to the earrings if desired using liver of sulfur and following the manufacturer's directions.

PEARL CUPS

Page 43   Length: 1¾"

Instructions

1. Place a flat disc in a dapping block. Put a dapping punch on top of the disc and hit it a couple times with a hammer. Put the disc in a smaller spot on the block, if you want more curve to the cup. Repeat with the remaining silver discs.

2. Punch holes in the center of the cups using a metal hole punch.

3. Make a wrapped loop at the end of one of the wire pieces. String an 8 mm pearl on the remaining end of the wire and begin a wrapped loop on top.

4. String the loop through an end link of a piece of chain and complete the wrap to secure.

5. String a 4 mm pearl and a cup onto a head pin, so the pearl is nestled into the cup. Begin a wrapped loop on top of the cup.

6. String the loop through the last link of the chain and complete the wrap. Repeat to make and attach 1 more cup and pearl dangle to the same chain link.

7. Make 2 more cup-and-pearl dangles and attach them 1 link higher than the previous two.

8. Attach the dangle to the ear wire.

9. Repeat steps 3–8 to complete the second earring.

10. Add a patina finish to the earrings if desired using liver of sulfur and following the manufacturer's directions.

SILVER, AQUA, AND LAVENDER LEAF

Page 44   Length: 1½"

Instructions

1. Using needle-nose pliers, bend one eye pin about 1/16" from the loop using the leaf bead's "slope" as a guide to the correct angle. Bend the eye pin again even with the hole in the bead, so that the loop end is centered at the top of the leaf. String the leaf bead onto the wire and bend the wire a third time to make a triangle shape.

2. Grip the eye pin's loop with a pair of needle-nosed pliers, and with a second pair of pliers wrap the end of the eye pin around the ¹⁄₁₆" gap at the top of the leaf bead as for making a wire-wrapped bail.

3. String onto an eye pin: 1 daisy spacer, 1 aqua bead, 1 daisy spacer. Turn a plain loop on top.

4. Gently open the bottom loop of the aqua unit and string it through the loop of the leaf dangle. Close the loop to secure.

5. Attach the dangle to the ear wire.

6. Repeat steps 1–5 to complete the second earring.

CHAROITE AND TURQUOISE
Page 44   Length: 1⅛"

Instructions

String onto a head pin: 1 charoite barrel, 2 silver discs, 1 turquoise barrel. Make a wrapped loop on top, and then attach the dangle to the ear wire. Repeat to complete the second earring.

SIGNS OF SPRING
Page 45   Length: 2⅞"

Instructions

1. String a 4" length of silver wire through the middle hole of the ear wire and make a wrapped loop.

2. String a dichroic rondelle onto the wire and begin a wrapped loop. String the loop through the top loop of the "Blossom" stick and complete the wrap to secure.

3. String onto a head pin: 1 apatite chip, 1 Pixie bead, 1 dichroic rondelle. Begin a wrapped loop. Insert the loop through the bottom loop of the "Blossom" stick, making sure the Pixie bead face is facing front (the same as the "Blossom" stick). Complete the wrap to secure.

4. String 2 apatite chips onto a head pin and begin a wrapped loop. String the loop through a hole on one side of the ear wire and complete the wraps to secure. Repeat on the other side of the ear wire.

5. Repeat steps 1–4 to complete the second earring.

WATCH PART DANGLES
Page 45   Length: 3⅛"

Instructions

1. Gently open a 4 mm jump ring and string onto the loop of an ear wire and onto one of the end holes of a wheel bridge. Close the jump ring.

2. String 1 crimp tube on the beading wire, pass the wire through the same 4 mm jump ring back down through the crimp tube.

3. Holding the short end of the wire and the crimp bead with your nondominant hand, gently pull on the long end of the wire to tighten. Place the crimp bead in the back set of openings (closest to the hinge) of the crimping pliers. Position the crimp bead in the jaws with one wire on one side of the "lips" and the second wire on the other side of the "lips." Squeeze with the pliers. See illustration below.

4. Place the crimp bead in the front set of openings of the pliers, with the bead set on edge, like a crescent moon. Squeeze tightly to close the crimp and secure the wire ends inside the doubled-over bead. (Note: trim the excess wire after stringing on about ½" of beads.)

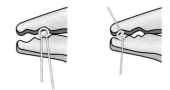

5. String onto the wire: 6 seed beads, 1 Pacific Opal round, 3 seed beads, 1 floral bead, one 4 mm Pacific Opal AB2 bicone, 1 Erinite SBL crystal bicone, 1 seed bead, 1 crimp tube. Crimp and trim.

6. String 1 crimp tube on the beading wire, pass the wire through the same 4 mm jump ring back down through the crimp tube. Pull the wire snug, crimp, and trim.

7. String onto the wire: 2 seed beads, 1 Pacific Opal round, 2 seed beads, 1 floral bead, 1 Pacific Opal AB2 bicone, 1 Erinite SBL bicone , 1 seed bead, 1 crimp tube. Crimp and trim.

8. String 1 crimp tube on the end of beading wire, crimp and trim. String the wire through: one 4 mm Indicolite AB2 bicone, the center hole on the wheel bridge, one 4 mm Indicolite AB2 bicone, 1 crimp tube. Pull the wire snug, crimp, and trim.

9. Gently open a 2.5 mm jump ring, string through the lower hole on the wheel bridge and through 1 fourth wheel. Close the ring to secure.

10. String onto a head pin: 1 seed bead, one 4 mm Indicolite bicone, 1 crown wheel, 1 seed bead, 1 Pacific Opal round. Insert the head pin into one side of JMC0308G bead frame, pass through one 6 mm Indicolite bicone, and then out the other side of the bead frame into 1 Smoked Topaz CAL spacer, 1 floral bead, 1 Tanzanite AB bicone, 1 Pacific Opal AB2 bicone.

11. Turn a plain loop on top. Gently open the loop and string onto the 2.5mm jump ring.

12. Repeat steps 1–11 to complete the second earring.

SEDONA SUNSET

Page 46   Length: 1¾"

Basic Peyote (Flat one-drop peyote stitch)

String on an even number of beads as indicated in the project instructions to make the first two rows. Start the third row by stringing on 1 bead and passing the needle through the second to last bead added in the initial group. String on 1 bead and pass the needle through the fourth to last bead added in the initial group. Continue in this manner skipping over a bead and inserting the needle into the previous bead until you reach the end of the first group of beads added. The upper edge of the peyote work will form an up-and-down pattern. For additional rows, add a bead at each "down" space and insert the needle through the bead creating the "up" in the pattern. For a flat piece of peyote that is 6 beads across, this means you would add only 3 beads (in the three down spaces) in each row.

Instructions

Refer to the Basic Peyote instructions as necessary when creating the peyote beads.

1. Thread a beading needle with approximately 1 yard of Fireline beading thread. String on 4 Delicas #1283 to create the first two rows of a peyote bead. Work in flat peyote stitch to make a piece 2 beads across by 16 rows long.

2. Roll the short ends together to make a tube. They will fit together like a zipper. Stitch the ends together to complete the bead.

3. Repeat steps 1 and 2 to make a total of 4 peyote-stitched tubular beads in #1283 (Tube A).

4. Make 8 peyote-stitched tubular beads, 2 beads across by 16 rows long as follows: String on 1 Delica #734, 2 Delicas #204, 1 Delica #734. Continue colors in lengthwise stripes (Tube B).

5. Make 4 peyote-stitched tubular beads, 2 beads across by 16 rows long using Delica #1014 (Tube C).

6. Make 4 peyote-stitched tubular beads, 1 bead across by 16 rows long using Delica #1014 (Tube D).

7. Make 2 peyote-stitched tubular beads, 5 beads across by 16 rows long as follows: String on 1 Delica #204, 2 Delicas #1283, 1 Delica #734, 2 Delicas #1014, 1 Delica #734, 2 Delicas #1283, 1 Delica #204. Continue the color pattern in lengthwise stripes (Tube E).

8. To assemble the earrings start on the end of an earring hoop with the v-notch. Wrap the sterling silver wire around the earring hoop 6 times. Trim the wire pressing the ends in to complete a wire coil. String on 1 Tube A. Continue adding wire coils and tubular peyote beads in the following order: copper wire coil, 1 Tube B, gun metal wire coil, 1 Tube C, sterling silver wire coil, 1 Tube B, copper wire coil, 1 Tube D, gun metal wire coil, 1 Tube E, gun metal wire coil, 1 Tube D, copper wire coil, 1 Tube B, sterling silver wire coil, 1 Tube C, gun metal wire coil, 1 Tube B, copper wire coil, 1 Tube A, sterling silver wire coil.

9. Repeat step 8 to complete the second earring.

CRAZY LONG

Page 46   Length: 2¼"

Instructions

1. String onto a head pin: 1 copper round, 1 fancy oval. Make a wrapped loop on top.

2. String onto an eye pin: 1 copper round, 1 crazy agate, 1 copper round. Make a wrapped loop on top.

3. Gently open the loop at the bottom of the crazy agate unit. String the fancy copper unit onto the loop and close the loop to secure. Attach the dangle to the ear wire.

4. Repeat steps 1–3 to complete the second earring.

SUNBURST

Page 47   Length: 1"

Instructions

Attach the Sunburst unit to an ear wire. Repeat to complete the second earring.

ARTISAN

Page 47   Length: 1⅛"

Instructions

String onto a head pin: 1 round, 1 bead cap, 1 lampworked bead, 1 bead cap, 1 round. Make a wrapped loop on top, and then attach the dangle to the ear wire. Repeat to complete the second earring.

NUTCRACKER

Page 48   Length: 1"

Instructions

String onto a head pin: 1 cube, 1 spacer, 1 round. Turn a plain loop on top. Gently open the plain loop, attach to the ear wire, and close the loop to secure. Repeat to complete the second earring.

RED AND MUSTARD YELLOW WITH BLACK DOTS

Page 48   Length: 1⅛"

Instructions

1. String onto a head pin: 1 crystal bicone, 1 spacer, 1 lampworked bead, 1 spacer, 1 crystal bicone. If the hole in the lampworked bead is large and the spacer doesn't stay centered, add a dot of jeweler's cement to the bead to secure each spacer in place.

2. Turn a plain loop on top of the beads. Open the plain loop, attach the ear wire, and close the loop to secure.

3. Repeat steps 1 and 2 to complete the second earring.

RED BONE TEARDROPS

Page 49   Length: 2⅝"

Instructions

1. Cut the wire into the following lengths:
   - 2 pieces, 2½"
   - 4 pieces, 1¼"

2. Turn a plain loop in one end of the 2½" length of wire. String onto the wire: 1 teardrop, 1 cone. Make a wrapped loop on top.

3. Turn a plain loop in one end of a 1¼" length of wire. String on 1 rondelle and turn a plain loop on top. Repeat this step.

4. Gently open a loop on one of the rondelles, attach to the second rondelle, and close the loop.

5. Open the loop on the bottom of the teardrop, attach the rondelle pair, and close the loop to secure.

6. Attach the dangle to the ear wire.

7. Repeat steps 2–6 to complete the second earring.

AGATE PICTURE FRAMES

Page 49   Length: 2⅝"

Instructions

1. String 1 jade rondelle onto a rope-and-dot head pin and begin a wrapped loop on top. String the loop through an end link of a piece of chain and complete the wrap.

2. Insert a plain head pin from the inside bottom of the picture frame bead so it exits on the outside. Make a wrapped loop. Repeat at the top of the picture frame bead.

3. Gently open the jump ring, string through the end link of the chain, and the loop at the bottom of the picture frame bead. Close the ring to secure.

4. Attach the dangle to the ear wire.

5. Repeat steps 1–4 to complete the second earring.

COPPER SWIRLS

Page 50   Length: 1¾"

Instructions

String onto a head pin: 1 pearl, 1 rondelle, 1 copper coin, 1 rondelle, 1 pearl. Make a wrapped loop on top, and then attach the dangle to the ear wire. Repeat to complete the earring.

LAMPWORK WITH PEARLS

Page 50   Length: 1⅛"

Instructions

String onto a head pin: 1 pearl, 1 spacer, 1 lampworked bead, 1 spacer. Make a wrapped loop on top, and then attach the dangle to the ear wire. Repeat to complete the second earring.

MOTTLED COINS

Page 51   Length: 1¼"

Instructions

String onto a head pin: 1 spacer, 1 coin, 1 spacer, 1 pearl. Make a wrapped loop on top, and then attach the dangle to the ear wire. Repeat to complete the second earring.

CELTIC

Page 51   Length: 1¼"

Instructions

1. Gently open the loop on an ear wire. String a Celtic link unit onto the loop and close the loop to secure.

2. String onto a head pin: 1 Jonquil bicone, 1 Olivine bicone. Begin a wrapped loop.

3. String the loop through the bottom loop of the Celtic link and complete the wraps to secure.

4. Repeat steps 1–3 to complete the second earring.

MARTINI AND OLIVE ART BEADS

Page 52   Length: 2¼"

Instructions

1. String onto a head pin: 1 crystal round, the olive art bead, 1 crystal round. Make a wrapped loop on top.

2. Trim the head off of a head pin. Begin a wrapped loop on one end, string the loop through the loop at the top of the olive dangle, and complete the wrap.

3. String onto the wire: 1 crystal round, 1 Czech faceted round. Make a wrapped loop on top.

4. Attach the dangle to the ear wire.

5. String the martini art bead to the middle of the 7" length of wire. Using your fingers and a pair of chain-nose pliers, bend the wire closely outlining the form of the bead.

6. On one of the wires, directly above and in the middle of the bead, bend the wire upward at a 90° angle using chain-nose pliers.

7. With the other end of the wire, make approximately 3 wraps around the vertical wire. Trim excess wrapping wire.

8. String a crystal round and a Czech faceted round onto the wire and make a wrapped loop on top.

9. Trim the head off of the remaining head pin. Begin a wrapped loop on one end, string the loop through the loop in the martini dangle and complete the wrap.

10. String a crystal round onto the head pin and make a wrapped loop on top. Attach the dangle to the ear wire.